The Poetry of Aphra Behn

Volume I – Poems Upon Several Occasions

Aphra Behn was a prolific and well established writer but facts about her remain scant and difficult to confirm. What can safely be said though is that Aphra Behn is now regarded as a key English playwright and a major figure in Restoration theatre

Aphra was born into the rising tensions to the English Civil War. Obviously a time of much division and difficulty as the King and Parliament, and their respective forces, came ever closer to conflict.

There are claims she was a spy, that she travelled abroad, possibly as far as Surinam.

By 1664 her marriage was over (though by death or separation is not known but presumably the former as it occurred in the year of their marriage) and she now used Mrs Behn as her professional name.

Aphra now moved towards pursuing a more sustainable and substantial career and began work for the King's Company and the Duke's Company players as a scribe.

Previously her only writing had been poetry but now she would become a playwright. Her first, "The Forc'd Marriage", was staged in 1670, followed by "The Amorous Prince" (1671). After her third play, "The Dutch Lover", Aphra had a three year lull in her writing career. Again it is speculated that she went travelling again, possibly once again as a spy.

After this sojourn her writing moves towards comic works, which prove commercially more successful. Her most popular works included "The Rover" and "Love-Letters Between a Nobleman and His Sister" (1684–87).

With her growing reputation Aphra became friends with many of the most notable writers of the day. This is The Age of Dryden and his literary dominance.

From the mid 1680's Aphra's health began to decline. This was exacerbated by her continual state of debt and descent into poverty.

Aphra Behn died on April 16th 1689, and is buried in the East Cloister of Westminster Abbey. The inscription on her tombstone reads: "Here lies a Proof that Wit can never be Defence enough against Mortality." She was quoted as stating that she had led a "life dedicated to pleasure and poetry."

Index of Contents

A Decicatory Epistle To the Right Honourable, JAMES, Earl of Salisbury, Viscount Cramborn, and Baron of Islington.

MY LORD,

Who should one celebrate with Verse and Song, but the Great, the Noble and the Brave? where dedicate an Isle of Love, but to the Gay, the Soft and Young? and who amongst Men can lay a better claim to these than Your Lordship? who like the Sun new risen with the early Day, looks round the World and sees nothing it cannot claim an interest in (for what cannot Wit, Beauty, Wealth and Honour claim?) The violent storms of Sedition and Rebellion are hush'd and calm'd; black Treason is retir'd to its old abode, the dark Abyss of Hell; the mysterious Riddles of Politick Knaves and Fools, which so long amused and troubled the World's repose, are luckily unfolded; and Your Lordship is saluted at Your first coming forth, Your first setting out for the glorious and happy Race of Life, by a Nation all glad, gay and smiling; and you have nothing before you but a ravishing prospect of eternal Joys, and everlasting inviting Pleasures, and all that Love and Fortune can bestow on their darling Youth, attend You in the noble persuit; and nothing can prevent Your being the most happy of her Favourites, but a too eager flight, a too swift speed o'er the charming flowry Meads and Plains that lie in view, between Your setting out and the end of Your glorious Chase. A long and illustrious race of Nobility has attended Your great Name, but none I believe ever came into the World with Your Lordship's advantages; amongst which, my Lord, 'tis not the least that You have the glory to be truly Loyal, and to be adorn'd with those excellent Principles, which render Nobility so absolutely worth the Veneration which is paid 'em; 'tis those. my Lord, and not the Title that make it truly great: Grandeur in any other serves but to point em out more particularly to the World, and shew their Faults with the greater magnitude, and render 'em more liable to contempt and that Reward which justly persues Ingratitude; nor is it, my Lord, the many unhappy Examples this Age has produc'd that has deter'd you from herding with the busie Unfortunates, and bringing Your powerful aid to their detestable cause, but a noble Honesty in Your Nature, a Generosity in Your Soul. That even part of Your Education had the good fortune not to be able to corrupt; no Opinion cou'd byass You, no Precedent debauch You; though all the fansied Glories of Power were promis'd You, though all the Contempt thrown on good and brave Men. all the subtile Arguments of the old Serpent, were us'd against the best of Kings and his illustrious Successour, still You were unmov'd; Your young stout Heart with a Gallantry and Force unusual resisted and defied the gilded Bait, laugh'd at the industrious Politicks of the busie Wise, and stubbornly Loyal, contemn'd the Counsels of the Grave. Go on, my Lord, advance in Noble resolution, grow up in strength of Loyalty, settle it about Your Soul, root it therellike the first Principles of Religion, which nothing ever throughly defaces, and which in spight of even Reason the Soul retains, whatever little Debaucheries the Tongue may commit; You that are great, are born the Bulwarks of sacred Majesty, its defence against all the storms of Fate, the Safety of the People in the Supporters of the Throne; and sure none that ever obey'd the Laws of God and the Dictates of Honour ever paid those Duties to a Sovereign that more truly merited the Defence and Adorations of his People than this of ours; and tis a blessing (since we are oblig'd to render it to the worst of Tyrant Kings) that we have one who so well justifies that intire Love and Submission we ought to pay him. You, my Lord, are one whom Thousands of good Men look up to with wondrous Veneration and Joy, when 'tis said Your Lordship amongst Your other Vertues is Loyal too, a true Tory! (a word of Honour now, the Royal Cause has sanctified it,) and though Your Lordship needs no encouragement to a good that rewards it self, yet I am confident You are not onely rank'd in the esteem of the best of Monarchs, but we shall behold you as one of our Preservers, and all England as one of its great Patrons, when Ages that shall come shall find Your noble Name inroll'd amongst the Friends to Monarchy in an Age of so villainous Corruption: Yes, my Lord, they will find it there and bless You. 'Tis this, my Lord, with every other Grace and Noble Vertue that adorns You, and gives the World such promises of Wonders in You, that makes me ambitious to be the first in the Croud of Your Admirers, that shall have the honour to celibrate Your great Name. Be pleased then, my Lord, to accept this Little Piece, which lazy Minutes begot and hard Fate has oblig'd me to bring forth into the censuring World, to which if any thing can reconcile it, 'twill be the glory it has to bear Your Noble Name in the front, and to be Patronized by so great and good a Man: Permit but my Zeal for Your Lordship to attone for the rest of my Faults, and Your Lordship will extremely oblige,

My Lord,
Your Lordship's most Humble,
and most Obedient Servant,

A. BEHN.

To Mrs. BEHN, on the Publishing Her Poems.

Madam,

Long has Wit's injur'd Empire been opprest
By Rhiming Fools, this Nations common Jest,
And sunk beneath the weight of heavy stafes,
In Tory Ballads and Whig Epitaphs;
The Ogs and Doegs reign'd, nay Baxter s zeal,
Has not been wanting too in writing Ill;
Yet still in spight of what the dull can doe,
'Tis here asserted and adorned by you.
This Book come forth, their credit must decay,
Ill Spirits vanish at th' approach of day:
And justly we before your envy'd feet,
There where our Hearts are due our Pens submit;
Ne'er to resume the baffled things again,
Unless in Songs of Triumph to thy Name;
Which are outdone by every Verse of thine,
Where thy own Fame does with more lustre shine,
Than all that we can give who in thy Praises join.
Fair as the face of Heaven, when no thick Cloud

Or darkning Storm the glorious prospect shroud;
In all its beauteous parts shines thy bright style
And beyond Humane Wit commends thy skill;
With all the thought and vigour of our Sex
The moving softness of your own you mix.
The Queen of Beauty and the God of Wars
Imbracing lie in thy due temper'd Verse,
Venus her sweetness and the force of Mars.
Thus thy luxuriant Muse her pleasure takes,
As God of old in Eden's blissful walks;
The Beauties of her new Creation view'd,
Full of content She sees that it is good.

Come then you inspir'd Swains and join your verse,
Though all in vain to add a Fame to hers;
But then your Song will best Apollo please,
When it is fraight with this his Favourite's praise.
Declare how when her learned Harp she strung,
Our joyfull Island with the Musick rung;
Descending Graces left their Heavenly seat,
To take their place in every Line she writ;
Where sweetest Charms as in her Person smile,
Her Face's Beauty's copy'd in her style.
Say how as she did her just skill improve
In the best Art and in soft Tales of Love.
Some well sung Passion with success she crown'd,
The melting Virgins languished at the sound.
And envying Swains durst not the Pipe inspire,
They'd nothing then to doe but to admire.
Shepherds and Nymphs, to Pan direct your Prayer,
If peradventure he your Vows will hear,
To make you sing, and make you look like her.
But, Nymphs and Swains, your hopes are al in vain,
For such bright Eyes, and such a tunefull Pen.

How many of her Sex spend half their days,
To catch some Fool by managing a Face?
But she secure of charming has confin'd
Her wiser care t' adorn and dress the Mind.
Beauty may fade, but everlasting Verse
Exempts the better portion from the Hearse.
The matchless Wit and Fancy of the Fair,
Which moves our envy and our Sons despair.
Long they shall live a monument of her Fame,
And to Eternity extend her Name;
While After-times deservedly approve
The choicest object of this Ages Love.
For when they reade, ghessing how far she charm'd,
With that bright Body with such Wit inform'd;
They will give heed and credit to our Verse,
When we the Wonders of her Face rehearse.

J. Cooper.
Buckden, Nov. 25, 1683.

To ASTRAEA, on Her Poems.

'Tis not enough to reade and to admire,
Thy sacred Verse does nobler thoughts inspire,
Striking on every breast Poetick fire:
The God of Wit attends with chearfull Rays,
Warming the dullest Statue into praise.
Hail then, delight of Heaven and pride of Earth,
Blest by each Muse at thy auspicious birth;
Soft Love and Majesty have fram'd thy Mind,
To shew the Beauties of both Sexes join'd:
Thy Lines may challenge, like young David's face,
A Female Sweetness and a Manly Grace;
Thy tender notions in loose numbers flow,
With a strange power to charm where e'er they go:
And when in stronger sounds thy voice we hear,
At all the skilfull points you arm'd appear.
Which way so'er thou dost thy self express,
We find thy Beauty out in every dress;
Such work so gently wrought, so strongly fine,
Cannot be wrought by hands all Masculine.
In vain proud Man weak Woman wou'd controul,
No Man can argue now against a Woman's Soul.

J. C.

To the Excellent Madam Behn, on Her Poems.

'Twas vain for Man the Laurels to persue,
(E'en from the God of Wit bright Daphne flew)
Man, Whose course compound damps the Muses fire,
It does but touch our Earth and soon expire;
While in the softer kind th' Aetherial flame,
Spreads and rejoices as from Heaven it came:
This Greece in Sappho, in Orinda knew
Our Isle; though they were but low types to you;
But the faint dawn to your illustrious day,
To make us patient of your brighter Ray.

Oft may we see some wretched story told;
In ductile sense spread thin as leaves of Gold.
You have ingrost th'inestimable Mine;
Which in well polisht Numbers you refine,

While still the solid Mass shines thick in every _ne.

Yet neither sex do you surpass alone,
Both in your Verse are in their glory shown,
Both Phoebus and Minerva are your own.
While in the softest dress you Wit dispense,
With all the Nerves of Reason and of Sense.
In mingled Beauties we at once may trace
A Female Sweetness and a Manly Grace.
No wonder 'tis the Delphian God of old
Wou'd have his Oracles by Women told.
But oh! who e'er so sweetly could repeat
Soft lays of Love, and youths delightfull heat?
If Love's Misfortunes be your mournfull Theme,
No dying Swan on fair Cayster's stream,
Expires so sweet, though with his numerous Moan,
The fading Banks and suffering Mountains groan.
If you the gentle Passions wou'd inspire,
With what resistless Charms you breathe desire?
No Heart so savage, so relentless none,
As can the sweet Captivity disown:
Ah, needs must she th'unwary Soul surprise
Whose Pen sheds Flames as dangerous as her Eyes.

J. Adams.

To the Authour, on Her Voyage to the Island of Love.

To speak of thee no Muse will I invoke,
Thou onely canst inspire what shou'd be spoke;
For all their wealth the Nine have given to thee,
Thy rich and flowing stream has left them dry:
Cupid may throw away his useless Darts,
Thou'st lent him one will massacre more Hearts
Than all his store, thy Pen disarms us so,
We yield our selves to the first beauteous Foe;
The easie softness of thy thoughts surprise,
And this new way Love steals into our Eyes;
Thy gliding Verse comes on us unawares,
No rumbling Metaphors alarm our Ears,
And puts us in a posture of defence;
We are undone and never know from whence.
So to th' Assyrian Camp the Angel flew,
And in the silent Night his Millions slew.
Thou leadst us by the Soul amongst thy Loves,
And bindst us all in thy inchanting Groves;
Each languishes for thy Aminta's Charms.
Sighs for thy fansied Raptures in her Arms,
Sees her in all that killing posture laid,

When Love and fond Respect guarded the sleeping Maid,
Persues her to the very Bower of Bliss,
Times all the wrecking joys and thinks 'em his;
In the same Trance with the young pair we lie,
And in their amorous Ecstasies we die.
You Nymphs, who deaf to Love's soft lays have been,
Reade here, and suck the sweet destruction in:
Smooth is the stream and clear is every thought,
And yet you cannot see with what you're caught;
Or else so very pleasing is the Bait,
With careless heed you play and leap at it:
She poisons all the Floud with such an art,
That the dear Philter trickles to the Heart,
With such bewitching pleasure that each sup
Has all the joys of life in every drop.
I see the Banks with Love-sick Virgins strow'd,
Their Bosoms heav'd with the young fluttering Gods;
Oh, how they pant and struggle with their pain!
Yet cannot wish their former health again:
Within their Breasts thy warmth and spirit glows,
And in their Eyes thy streaming softness flows;
Thy Raptures are transfus'd through every vein,
And thy blest hour in all their heads does reign;
The Ice that chills the Soul thou dost remove,
And meltst it into tenderness and Love;
The flints about their Hearts dance to thy lays,
Till the quick motion sets 'em on a Blaze.
Orpheus and you the stones do both inspire,
But onely you out of those flints strike fire,
Not with a sudden Spark, a short liv'd Blaze,
Like Womens Passions in our Gilting days;
But what you fire burns with a constant flame,
Like what you write, and always is the same.
Rise, all ye weeping Youth, rise and appear,
Whom gloomy Fate has damn'd to black Despair;
Start from the ground and throw your Mourning by,
Loves great Sultana says you shall not die:
The dismal dark half year is over past,
The Sea is op'd, the Sun shines out at last,
And Trading's free, the storms are husht as death,
Or happy Lovers ravisht out of breath;
And listen to Astrteas Harmony,
Such power has elevated Poetry.

T.C.

"To the Lovely Witty ASTRAEA, on Her Excellent Poems.

Oh, wonder of thy Sex! Where can we see,

Beauty and Knowledge join'd except in thee?
Such pains took Nature with your Heav'nly Face,
Form'd it for Love, and moulded every Grace;
I doubted first and fear'd that you 'had been
Unfinish'd left like other She's within:
I see the folly of that fear, and find
Your Face is not more beauteous than your Mind:
Whoe'er beheld you with a Heart unmov'd,
That sent not sighs, and said within he lov'd?
I gaz'd and found, a then, unknown delight,
Life in your looks, and Death to leave the sight.
What joys, new Worlds of joys has he possest.
That gain'd the sought-for welcome of your Breast?

Your Wit wou'd recommend the homeliest Face,
Your Beauty make the dullest Humour please;
But where they both thus gloriously are join'd,
All Men submit, you reign in every Mind.
What Passions does your Poetry impart?
It shews th'unfathom'd thing a Woman's Heart,
Tells what Love is, his Nature and his Art,
Displays the several Scenes of Hopes and Fears,
Love's Smiles, his Sighs, his Laughing and his Tears.
Each Lover here may reade his different Fate,
His Mistress kindness or her scornfull hate.
Come all whom the blind God has led astray
Here the bewildred Youth is shew'd his way:
Guided by this he may yet love and find
Ease in his Heart, and reason in his Mind.
Thus sweetly once the charming W------ lr strove
In Heavenly sounds to gain his hopeless Love:
All the World listned but his scornfull Fair,
Pride stopt her ears to whom he bent his prayer.

Much happier you that can't desire in vain
But what you wish as soon as wish'd obtain.

Upon These and Other Excellent Works of the Incomparable ASTRAEA.

I.
Ye bold Magicians in Philosophy,
That vainly think (next the Almighty three)
The brightest Cherubin in all the Hierarchy
Will leave that Glorious Sphere
And to your wild inchantments will appear;
To the fond summons of fantastick Charms,
As Barbarous and inexplicable Terms:
As those the trembling Sorcerer dreads,
When he the Magick Circle treads:

And as he walks the Mystick rounds,
And mutters the detested sounds,
The Stygian fiends exalt their wrathfull heads;
And all ye bearded Drudges of the Schools,
That sweat in vain to mend predestin'd fools,
With senseless Jargon and perplexing Rules;
Behold and with amazement stand,
Behold a blush with shame and wonder too,
What Divine Nature can in Woman doe.
Behold if you can see in all this fertile Land
Such an Anointed head, such an inspired hand.

II.

Rest on in peace, ye blessed Spirits, rest,
With Imperial bliss for ever blest:
Upon your sacred Urn she scorns to tread,
Or rob the Learned Monuments of the dead:
Nor need her Muse a foreign aid implore,
In her own tunefull breast there's wonderous store.
Had she but flourisht in these times of old,
When Mortals were amongst the Gods inrolld,
She had not now as Woman been Ador'd,
But with Diviner sacrifice Implor'd;
Temples and Altars had preserved her name
And she her self been thought Immortal as her fame.

III.

Curst be the balefull Tongue that dares abuse
The rightfull off-spring of her Godlike Muse:
And doubly Curst be he that thinks her Pen
Can be instructed by the best of men.
The times to come (as surely she will live,
As many Ages as are past,
As long as Learning, Sense, or wit survive,
As long as the first principles of Bodies last.)
The future Ages may perhaps believe
One soft and tender Arm cou'd ne'er atchieve
The wonderous deeds that she has done
So hard a prize her Conqu'ring Muse has won.
But we that live in the great Prophetesses days
Can we enough proclaim her praise,
We that experience every hour
The blest effects of her Miraculous power?
To the sweet Musick of her charming tongue,
In numerous Crowds the ravisht hearers throng:
And even a Herd of Beasts as wild as they
That did the Thracian Lyre obey,
Forget their Madness and attend her song.
The tunefull Shepherds on the dangerous rocks
Forsake their Kinds and leave their bleating Flocks,

And throw their tender Reeds away,
As soon as e'er her softer Pipe begins to play.
No barren subject, no unfertile soil
Can prove ungratefull to her Muses Toil,
Warm'd with the Heavenly influence of her Brain,
Upon the dry and sandy plain,
On craggy Mountains cover'd o'er with Snow,
The blooming Rose and fragrant Jes'min grow:
When in her powerful Poetick hand,
She waves the mystick wand,
Streight from the hardest Rocks the sweetest numbers flow.

IV.
Hail bright Urania! Erato hail!
Melpomene, Polymnia, Euterpe, hail!
And all ye blessed powers that inspire
The Heaven-born Soul with intellectual fire;
Pardon my humble and unhallow'd Muse,
If she too great a veneration use,
And prostrate at your best lov'd Darling's feet
Your holy Fane with sacred honour greet:
Her more than Pythian Oracles are so divine
You sure not onely virtually are
Within the glorious Shrine,
But you your very selves must needs be there.
The Delian Prophet did at first ordain,
That even the mighty Nine should reign,
In distant Empires of different Clime;
And if in her triumphant Throne,
She rules those learned Regions alone,
The fam'd Pyerides are out-done by her omnipotent Rhime.
In proper Cells her large capacious Brain
The images of all things does contain,
As bright almost as were th' Ideas laid,
In the last model e'er the World was made.
And though her vast conceptions are so strong,
The powerfull eloquence of her charming tongue
Does, clear as the resistless beams of day,
To our enlightned Souls the noble thoughts convey
Well chosen, well appointed, every word
Does its full force and natural grace afford
And though in her rich treasury,
Confus'd like Elements great Numbers lie,
When they their mixture and proportion take,
What beauteous forms of every kind they make!
Such was the Language God himself infus'd,
And such the style our great Forefather us'd,
From one large stock the various sounds he fram'd,
And every Species of the vast Creation nam'd.
While most of our dull Sex have trod
In beaten paths of one continued Road,

Her skilfull and well manag'd Muse
Does all the art and strength of different paces use:
For though sometimes with slackned force,
She wisely stops her fleetest course,
That slow but strong Majestick pace
Shews her the swiftest steed of all the chosen Race.

V.

Well has she sung the learned Daphnis praise,
And crown'd his Temple with immortal Bays;
And all that reade him must indeed confess,
Th'effects of such a cause could not be less.
For ne'er was (at the first bold heat begun)
So hard and swift a Race of glory run,
But yet her sweeter Muse did for him more,
Than he himself or all Apollo's sons before;
For shou'd th' insatiate lust of time
Root out the memory of his sacred Rhime,
The polish'd armour in that single Page
Wou'd all the tyranny and rage
Of Fire and Sword defie,
For Daphnis can't but with Astrtea die.
And who can dark oblivion fear,
That is co-eval with her mighty Works and Her?
Ah learned Chymist, 'tis she onely can
By her almighty arm,
Within the pretious salt collect,
The true essential form,
And can against the power of death protect
Not onely Herbs and Trees, but raise the buried Man.

VI.

Wretched (Enonis inauspicious fate,
That she was born so soon, or her blest Muse so late!
Cou'd the poor Virgin have like her complain'd,
She soon her perjur'd Lover had regain'd,
In spight of all the fair Seducers tears,
In spight of all her Vows and Prayers;
Such tender accents through his Soul had ran,
As wou'd have pierc'd the hardest heart of Man.
At every Line the fugitive had swore
By all the Gods, by all the Powers divine,
My dear (Enone, I'll be ever thine,
And ne'er behold the flattering Grecian more.
How does it please the learned Roman's Ghost
(The sweetest that th' Ely si an Field can boast)
To see his noble thoughts so well exprest,
So tenderly in a rough Language drest;
Had she there liv'd, and he her Genius known,
So soft, so charming, and so like his own,
One of his Works had unattempted been,

And Ovid ne'er in mournfull Verse been seen;
Then the great Ctesar to the Scythian plain,
From Rome's gay Court had banish'd him in vain,
Her plenteous Muse had all his wants supplied.
And he had flourish'd in exalted pride:
No barbarous Getans had deprav'd his tongue,
For he had onely listned to her Song,
Not as an exile, but proscrib'd by choice,
Pleas'd with her Form, and ravish'd with her voice.
His last and dearest part of Life,
Free from noise and glorious strife,
He there had spent within her softer Armes,
And soon forgot the Royal Julia's charmes.

VII.
Long may she scourge this mad rebellious Age,
And stem the torrent of Fanatick rage,
That once had almost overwhelmed the Stage.
O'er all the Land the dire contagion spread,
And e'en Apollo's Sons apostate fled:
But while that spurious race imploy'd their parts
In studying strategems and subtile arts,
To alienate their Prince's Subjects hearts,
Her Loyal Muse still tun'd her loudest strings,
To sing the praises of the best of Kings.
And, O ye sacred and immortal Gods,
From the blest Mansions of your bright aboeds,
To the first Chaos let us all be hurld,
E'er such vile wretches should reform the World,
That in all villany so far excell,
If they in sulphurous flames must onely dwell,
The Cursed Caitiffs hardly merit Hell.
Were not those vile Achitophels so lov'd,
(The blind, the senseless and deluded Crowd)
Did they but half his Royal Vertues know,
But half the blessings which to him they owe,
His long forbearance to provoking times,
And God-like mercy to the worst of crimes:
Those murmuring SJrimei's) even they alone,
Cou'd they bestow a greater than his own.
Wou'd from a Cottage raise him to a Throne.

VIII.
See, ye dull Scriblers of this frantick Age,
That load the Press, and so overwhelm the Stage,
That e'en the noblest art that e'er was known,
As great as an Egyptian Plague is grown:
Behold, ye scrawling Locusts, what ye've done,
What a dire judgment is brought down,
By your curst Dogrel Rhimes upon the Town;
On Fools and Rebels hangs an equal Fate,

And both may now repent too late,
For the great Charter of your Wit as well as Trade is gone.
Once more the fam'd Astraea's come;
'Tis she pronounc'd the fatal doom,
And has restor'd it to the rightfull Heirs,
Since Knowledge first in Paradise was theirs.

IX.
Never was Soul and Body better joyn'd,
A Mansion worthy of so blest a Mind;
See but the Shadow of her beauteous face,
The pretious minitures of every Grace,
There one may still such Charms behold,
That as Idolaters of old,
The works of their own hands ador'd,
And Gods which they themselves had made implor'd;
Jove might again descend below,
And, with her Wit and Beauty charm'd, to his own Image bow.
But oh, the irrevocable doom of Nature's Laws!
How soon the brightest Scene of Beauty draws!
Alas, what's all the glittering Pride
Of the poor perishing Creatures of a day,
With what a violent and impetuous Tide,
E'er they're flow'd in their glories ebb away?
The Pearl, the Diamond and Saphire must
Be blended with the common Pebbles dust,
And even Astrtea with all her sacred store,
Be wreckt on Death's inevitable Shore,
Her Face ne'er seen and her dear Voice be heard no more.
And wisely therefore e'er it was too late,
She has revers'd the sad Decrees of Fate,
And in deep Characters of immortal Wit,
So large a memorandum's writ,
That the blest memory of her deathless Name
Shall stand recorded in the Book of Fame;
When Towns inter'd in their own ashes lie,
And Chronicles of Empires die,
When Monuments like Men want. Tombs to tell
Where the remains of the vast ruines fell.

To the excellent ASTRAEA.

We all can well admire, few well can praise
Where so great merit does the Subject raise:
To write our Thoughts alike from dulness free,
On this hand, as on that from flattery;
He who wou'd handsomly the Medium hit,
Must have no little of Astraea's Wit.
Let others in the noble Task engage,

Call you the Phoenix, wonder of the Age,
The Glory of your Sex, the Shame of ours,
Crown you with Garlands of Rhetorick Flowers;
For me, alas, I nothing can design,
To render your soft Numbers more divine,
Than by comparison with these of mine:
As beauteous paintings are set off by shades,
And some fair Ladies by their dowdy Maids;
Yet after all, forgive me if I name
One Fault where, Madam, you are much to blame,
To wound with Beauty's fighting on the square,
But to o'ercome with Wit too is not fair;
'Tis like the poison'd Indian Arrows found,
For thus you're sure to kill where once you wound.

J.W.

To Madam A. Behn on the Publication of her Poems.

I.
When the sad news was spread,
The bright, the fair Orlndas dead,
We sigh'd, we mourn'd, we wept, we griev'd,
And fondly with our selves conceiv'd,
A loss so great could never be retriev'd.
The Ruddy Warriour laid his Truncheon by,
Sheath'd his bright sword, and glorious Arms forgot,
The sounds of Triumph, braggs of Victory,
Rais'd in his Breast no emulative thought;
For pond'ring on the common Lot,
Where is, said He the Difference in the Grave,
Betwixt the Coward and the Brave?
Since She, alas, whose inspired Muse should tell
To unborn Ages how the Hero fell,
From the Impoverisht Ignorant World is fled,
T'inhance the mighty mighty Number of the dead.

II.
The trembling Lover broke his tuneless Lure,
And said be thou for ever mute:
Mute as the silent shades of night,
Whither Qrindas gone,
Thy musicks best instructress and thy musicks song;
She that could make
Thy inarticulated strings to speak,
In language soft as young desires,
In language chaste as Vestal fires;
But she hath ta'n her Everlasting flight:
Ah! cruel Death,

How short's the date of Learned breath!
No sooner do's the blooming Rose,
Drest fresh and gay,
In the embroy 'dries of her Native May,
 Her odorous sweets expose,
But with thy fatal knife,
The fragrant flow'r is crop't from off the stalk of life.

III.

Come, ye Stoicks^ come away,
You that boast an Apathy,
And view our Golgotha;
See how the mourning Virgins all around,
With Tributary Tears bedew the sacred ground;
And tell me, tell me where's the Eye
That can be dry,
Unless in hopes (nor are such hopes in vain)
Their universal cry,
Should mount the vaulted sky,
And of the Gods obtain,
A young succeeding Phoenix might arise
From Orindas spicy obsequies.
In Heaven the voice was heard,
Heaven does the Virgins pray'rs regard;
And none that dwells on high,
If once the beauteous Ask, the beauteous can deny.

IV.

'Tis done, 'tis done, th' imperial grant is past,
We have our wish at last,
And now no more with sorrow be it said,
Orindas dead;
Since in her seat Astrtea does Appear,
The God of Wit has chosen her,
To bear Orlnda's and his Character.
The Laurel Chaplet seems to grow
On her more gracefull Brow;
And in her hand
Look how she waves his sacred Wand:
Loves Quiver's tyde
In an Azure Mantle by her side,
And with more gentle Arts
Than he who owns the Aureal darts,
At once she wounds, and heals our hearts.

V.

Hark how the gladded Nymphs rejoyce,
And with a gracefull voice,
Commend Apollo s Choice.
The gladded Nymphs their Guardian Angel greet,
And chearfully her name repeat,

And chearfully admire and praise,
The Loyal musick of her layes;
Whilst they securely sit,
Beneath the banners of her wit,
And scorn th'ill-manner'd Ignorance of those,
Whose Stock's so poor they cannot raise
To their dull Muse one subsidy of praise,
Unless they're dubb'd the Sexes foes,
These squibbs of sense themselves expose.
Or if with stolen light
They shine one night,
The next their earth-born Lineage shows,
They perish in their slime,
And but to name them, wou'd defile Astrtea's Rhime.

VI.
But you that would be truely wise,
And vertues fair Idea prize;
You that would improve
In harmless Arts of not indecent Love:
Arts that Romes fam'd Master never taught,
Or in the Shops of fortune's bought.
Would you know what Wit doth mean,
Pleasant wit yet not obscene,
The several garbs that Humours wear,
The dull, the brisk, the jealous, the severe?
Wou'd you the pattern see
Of spotless and untainted Loyalty,
Deck't in every gracefull word
That language that afford;
Tropes and Figures, Raptures and Conceits that ly,
Disperst in all the pleasant Fields of poesie?
Reade you then Astrteas lines,
'Tis in those new discover'd Mines,
Those golden Quarries that this Ore is founc
With which in Worlds as yet unknown Astrea shall be crown 'd.

VII.
And you th' Advent'rous sons of fame,
You that would sleep in honours bed
With glorious Trophies garnished;
You that with living labours strive
Your dying Ashes to survive;
Pay your Tributes to Astraea's name,
Her Works can spare you immortality,
For sure her Works shall never dye.
Pyramids must fall and Mausolean Monurrents decay,
Marble Tombs shall crumble into dust,
Noisie Wonders of a short liv'd day,
That must in time yield up their Trust;
And had e'er this been perisht quite

Ith' ruines of Eternal night,
Had no kind Pen like her's,
In powerfull numbers powerfull verse,
Too potent for the gripes of Avaritious fate,
To these our ages lost declared their pristine State.

VIII.
But time it self, bright Nymph, shall never conquer thee,
For when the Globe of vast Eternity;
Turns up the wrong-side of the World,
And all things are to their first Chaos hurl'd,
Thy lasting praise in thy own lines inroll'd,
With Roman and with the British Names shall Equal honour hold.
And surely none 'midst the Poetick Quire,
But justly will admire
The Trophies of thy wit,
Sublime and gay as e'er were yet
In Charming Numbers writ.
Or VirgiFs Shade or Ovid's Ghost,
Of Ages past the pride and boast;
Or Cow ley (first of ours) refuse
That thou shouldst be Companion of their Muse.
And if 'twere lawfull to suppose
(As where's the Crime or Incongruity)
Those awfull Souls concern'd can be
At any sublunary thing,
Alas, I fear they'll grieve to see,
That whilst I sing,
And strive to praise, I but disparage thee.

By F. N. W.

To Madam Behn, on Her Poems.

When th' Almighty Powers th' Universe had fram'd,
And Man as King, the lesser World was nam'd.
The Glorious Consult soon his joys did bless.
And sent him Woman his chief happiness.
She by an after-birth Heaven did refine,
And gave her Beauty with a Soul divine;
She with delight was Natures chiefest pride,
Dearer to Man than all the World beside;
Her soft embraces charm'd his Manly Soul,
And softer Words his Roughness did controul:
So thou, great Sappho, with thy charming Verse,
Dost here the Soul of Poetry rehearse;
From your sweet Lips such pleasant Raptures fell,
As if the Graces strove which shou'd excell.
Th'admiring World when first your Lute you strung.

Became all ravisht with th' immortal Song;
So soft and gracefull Love in you is seen,
As if the Muses had designed you Queen.
For thee, thou great Britannia of our Land,
How does thy Praise our tunefull Feet command?
With what great influence do thy Verses move?
How hast thou shewn the various sense of Love?
Admir'd by us, and blest by all above.
To you all tribute's due, and I can raise
No glory but by speaking in your praise.
Go on and bless us dayly with your Pen,
And we shall oft return thee thanks again.

H. Watson.

POEMS UPON SEVERAL OCCASIONS.

The Golden Age.

A Paraphrase on a Translation Out of French.

I.
Blest Age! when ev'ry Purling Stream
Ran undisturb'd and clear,
When no scorn'd Shepherds on your Banks were seen,
Tortur'd by Love, by Jealousie, or Fear;
When an Eternal Spring drest ev'ry Bough,
And Blossoms fell, by new ones dispossest;
These their kind Shade affording all below,
And those a Bed where all below might rest
The Groves appear'd all drest with Wreaths of Flowers,
And from their Leaves dropt Aromatick Showers,
Whose fragrant Heads in Mystick Twines above,
Exchang'd their Sweets, and mix'd with thousand Kisses,
As if the willing Branches strove
To beautifie and shade the Grove
Where the young wanton Gods of Love
Offer their Noblest Sacrifice of Blisses.

II.
Calm was the Air, no Winds blew fierce and loud,
The Skie was darkened with no sullen Cloud;
But all the Heav'ns laugh'd with continued Light,
And scattered round their Rays serenely bright.
No other Murmurs fill'd the Ear
But what the Streams and Rivers purl'd,
When Silver Waves o'er Shining Pebbles curl'd;
Or when young Zepkirs fan'd the Gentle Breez,
Gathering fresh Sweets from Balmy Flow rs and Trees,

Then bore 'em on their Wings to perfume all the Air:
While to their soft and tender Play,
The Gray-Plum'd Natives of the Shades
Unwearied sing till Love invades,
Then Bill, then sing agen, while Love and Musick makes the Day.

III.
The stubborn Plough had then,
Made no rude Rapes upon the Virgin Earth;
Who yielded of her own accord her plentious Birth,
Without the Aids of men;
As if within her Teeming Womb,
All Nature, and all Sexes lay,
Whence new Creations every day
Into the happy World did come:
The Roses fill'd with Morning Dew,
Bent down their loaded heads,
T'Adorn the careless Shepherds Grassy Beds
While still young opening Buds each moment grew
And as those withered, drest his shaded Couch a new;
Beneath who's boughs the Snakes securely dwelt,
Not doing harm, nor harm from others felt;
With whom the Nymphs did Innocently play,
No spightful Venom in the wantons lay;
But to the touch were Soft, and to the sight were Gay.

IV.
Then no rough sound of Wars Alarms,
Had taught the World the needless use of Arms:
Monarchs were uncreated then,
Those Arbitrary Rulers over men:
Kings that made Laws, first broke 'em, and the Gods
By teaching us Religion first, first set the World at Odds:
Till then Ambition was not known,
That Poyson to Content, Bane to Repose;
Each Swain was Lord o'er his own will alone,
His Innocence Religion was, and Laws.
Nor needed any troublesome defence
Against his Neighbours Insolence.
Flocks, Herds, and every necessary good
Which bounteous Nature had design'd for Food,
Whose kind increase o'er-spread the Meads and Plaines,
Was then a common Sacrifice to all th'agreeing Swaines.

V.
Right and Property were words since made,
When Power taught Mankind to invade:
When Pride and Avarice became a Trade;
Carri'd on by discord, noise and wars,
For which they bartered wounds and scarrs;
And to Inhaunce the Merchandize, miscall'd it, Fame,

And Rapes, Invasions, Tyrannies,
Was gaining of a Glorious Name:
Stiling their salvage slaughters, Victories;
Honour, the Error and the Cheat
Of the Ill-natur'd Bus'ey Great,
Nonsense, invented by the Proud,
Fond Idol of the slavish Crowd,
. Thou wert not known in those blest days
Thy Poyson was not mixt with our unbounded Joyes;
Then it was glory to pursue delight,
And that was lawful all, that Pleasure did invite,
Then 'twas the Amorous world injoy'd its Reign;
And Tyrant Honour strove t' usurp in Vain.

VI.
The flowry Meads, the Rivers and the Groves,
Were fill'd with little Gay-wing'd Loves:
That ever smil'd and danc'd and Play'd,
And now the woods, and now the streames invade,
And where they came all things were gay and glad:
When in the Myrtle Groves the Lovers sat
Opprest with a too fervent heat;
A Thousands Cupids fann'd their wings aloft,
And through the Boughs the yielded Ayre would waft:
Whose parting Leaves discovered all below,
And every God his own soft power admir'd,
And smil'd and fann'd, and sometimes bent his Bow;
Where e'er he saw a Shepherd uninspir'd.
The Nymphs were free, no nice, no coy disdain;
Deny'd their Joyes, or gave the Lover pain;
The yielding Maid but kind Resistance makes;
Trembling and blushing are not marks of shame,
But the Effect of kindling Flame:
Which from the sighing burning Swain she takes,
While she with tears all soft, and down-cast-eyes,
Permits the Charming Conqueror to win the prize.

VII.
The Lovers thus, thus uncontroul'd did meet,
Thus all their Joyes and Vows of Love repeat:
Joyes which were everlasting, ever new
And every Vow inviolably true:
Not kept in fear of Gods, no fond Religious cause,
Nor in obedience to the duller Laws.
Those Fopperies of the Gown were then not known,
Those vain, those Politick Curbs to keep man in,
Who by a fond mistake Created that a Sin;
Which freeborn we, by right of Nature claim our own.
Who but the Learned and dull moral Fool
Could gravely have forseen, man ought to live by Rule?

VIII.

Oh cursed Honour! thou who first didst damn,
A Woman to the Sin of shame;
Honour! that rob'st us of our Gust,
Honour! that hindred mankind first,
At Loves Eternal Spring to squench his amorous thirst.
Honour! who first taught lovely Eyes the art,
To wound, and not to cure the heart:
With Love to invite, but to forbid with Awe,
And to themselves prescribe a Cruel Law;
To Veil 'em from the Lookers on,
When they are sure the slave's undone,
And all the Charmingst part of Beauty hid;
Soft Looks, consenting Wishes, all deny'd.
It gathers up the flowing Hair,
That loosely plaid with wanton Air.
The Envious Net, and stinted order hold,
The lovely Curls of Jet and shining Gold;
No more neglected on the Shoulders hurl'd:
Now drest to Tempt, not gratify the World:
Thou, Miser Honour, hord'st the sacred store,
And starv'st thy self to keep thy Votaries poor.

IX.

Honour! that put'st our words that should be free
Into a set Formality.
Thou base Debaucher of the generous heart,
That teachest all our Looks and Actions Art;
What Love designed a sacred Gift,
What Nature made to be possest;
Mistaken Honour, made a Theft,
For Glorious Love should be confest:
For when confin'd, all the poor Lover gains,
Is broken Sighs, pale Looks, Complaints and Pains.
Thou Foe to Pleasure, Nature's worst Disease,
Thou Tyrant over mighty Kings,
What mak'st thou here in Shepheards Cottages;
Why troublest thou the quiet Shades and Springs?
Be gone, and make thy Fam'd resort
To Princes Pallaces;
Go Deal and Chaffer in the Trading Court,
That busie Market for Phantastick Things;
Be gone and interrupt the short Retreat,
Of the Illustrious and the Great;
Go break the Politicians sleep,
Disturb the Gay Ambitious Fool,
That longs for Scepters, Crowns, and Rule,
Which not his Title, nor his Wit can keep;
But let the humble honest Swain go on,
In the blest Paths of the first rate of man;
That nearest were to Gods Alii'd,

And form'd for love alone, disdain'd all other Pride.

X.
Be gone! and let the Golden age again,
Assume its Glorious Reign;
Let the young wishing Maid confess,
What all your Arts would keep conceal'd:
The Mystery will be reveal'd,
And she in vain denies, whilst we can guess,
She only shows the Jilt to teach man how,
To turn the false Artillery on the Cunning Foe.
Thou empty Vision hence, be gone,
And let the peaceful Swain love on;
The swift pac'd hours of life soon steal away:
Stint not, yee Gods, his short liv'd Joy.
The Spring decays, but when the Winter's gore,
The Trees and Flowers a new comes on;
The Sun may set, but when the night is fled,
And gloomy darkness does retire,
He rises from his Watry Bed:
All Glorious, Gay, all drest in Amorous Fire.
But Sylvia when your Beauties fade,
When the fresh Roses on your Cheeks shall die,
Like Flowers that wither in the Shade,
Eternally they will forgotten lye,
And no kind Spring their sweetness will supply.
When Snow shall on those lovely Tresses lye
And your fair Eyes no more shall give us pain,
But shoot their pointless Darts in vain.
What will your duller honour signifie?
Go boast it then! and see what numerous Store
Of Lovers will your Ruin'd Shrine Adore.
Then let us, Sylvia, yet be wise,
And the Gay hasty minutes prize:
The Sun and Spring receive but our short Light,
Once sett, a sleep brings an Eternal Night.

A Farewel to Celladon, On His Going into Ireland.

Pindarique.

Farewell the Great, the Brave and Good,
By all admir'd and understood;
For all thy vertues so extensive are,
Writ in so noble and so plain a Character,
That they instruct humanity what to do,
How to reward and imitate 'em too,
The mighty Cesar found and knew,
The Value of a Swain so true:

And early call'd the Industrious Youth from Groves
Where unambitiously he lay,
And knew no greater Joyes, nor Power then Loves;
Which all the day
The careless and delighted Celladon Improves;
So the first man in Paradice was laid,
So blest beneath his own dear fragrant shade,
Till false Ambition made him range,
So the Almighty call'd him forth,
And though for Empire he did Eden change;
Less Charming 'twas, and far less worth.

II.
Yet he obeyes and leaves the peaceful Plains,
The weeping Nymphs, and sighing Swains,
Obeys the mighty voice of Jove.
The Dictates of his Loyalty pursues,
Bus'ness Debauches all his hours of Love;
Bus'ness, whose hurry, noise and news
Even Natures self subdues;
Changes her best and first simplicity,
Her soft, her easie quietude
Into mean Arts of cunning Policy,
The Grave and Drudging Coxcomb to Delude.
Say, mighty Celladon, oh tell me why,
Thou dost thy nobler thoughts imploy
In business, which alone was made
To teach the restless Statesman how to Trade
In dark Cabals for Mischief and Design,
But n'ere was meant a Curse to Souls like thine.
Business the Check to Mirth and Wit,
Business the Rival of the Fair,
The Bane to Friendship, and the Lucky Hit,
Onely to those that languish in Dispair;
Leave then that wretched troublesome Estate
To him to whom forgetful Heaven,
Has no one other vertue given,
But dropt down the unfortunate,
To Toyl, be Dull, and to be Great.

III.
But thou whose nobler Soul was fram'd,
For Glorious and Luxurious Ease,
By Wit adorn'd, by Love inflam'd;
For every Grace, and Beauty Fam'd,
Form'd for delight, design'd to please,
Give, Give a look to every Joy,
That youth and lavish Fortune can invent,
Nor let Ambition, that false God, destroy
Both Heaven and Natures first intent.

But oh in vain is all I say,
And you alas must go,
The Mighty Casar to obey,
And none so fit as you.
From all the Envying Croud he calls you forth,
He knows your Loyalty, and knows your worth
He's try'd it oft, and put it to the Test,
It grew in Zeal even whilst it was opprest,
The great, the Godlike Celladon,
Unlike the base Examples of the times,
Cou'd never be Corrupted, never won,
To stain his honest blood with Rebel Crimes.
Fearless unmov'd he stood amidst the tainted Crowd,
And justify'd and own'd his Loyalty aloud.

IV.
Hyhernia hail! Hail happy Isle,
Be glad, and let all Nature smile.
Ye Meads and Plains send forth your Gayest Flowers;
Ye Groves and every Purling Spring,
Where Lovers sigh, and Birds do sing,
Be glad and gay, for Celladon is yours;
He comes, he comes to grace your Plains.
To Charm the Nymphs, and bless the Swains,
Ecchoes repeat his Glorious Name
To all the Neighbouring Woods and Hills;
Ye Feather'd Quire chant forth his Fame,
Ye Fountains, Brooks, and Wand'ring Rills,
That through the Meadows in Meanders rur,
Tell all your Flowry Brinks, the generous Swain is come.

VI.
Divert him all ye pretty Solitudes,
And give his Life some softning Interludes:
That when his weari'd mind would be,
From Noise and Rigid Bus'ness free;
He may upon your Mossey Beds lye down,
Where all is Gloomy, all is Shade,
With some dear Shee, whom Nature made,
To be possest by him alone;
Where the soft tale of Love She breathes,
Mixt with the rushing of the wind-blown leaves,
The different Notes of Cheerful Birds,
And distant Bleating of the Herds:
Is Musick far more ravishing and sweet,
Then all the Artful Sounds that please the noisey Great.

VII.
Mix thus your Toiles of Life with Joyes,
And for the publick good, prolong your days:
Instruct the World, the great Example prove,

Of Honour, Friendship, Loyalty, and Love.
And when your busier hours are done,
And you with Damon sit alone;
Damon the honest, brave and young;
Whom we must Celebrate where you are sung,
For you (by Sacred Friendship ty'd,)
Love nor Fate can nere divide;
When your agreeing thoughts shall backward run,
Surveying all the Conquests you have won,
The Swaines you'ave left, the sighing Maids undone;
Try if you can a fatal prospect take,
Think if you can a soft Idea make:
Of what we are, now you are gone,
Of what we feel for Celladon.

VIII.
'Tis Celladon the witty and the gay,
That blest the Night, and cheer'd the world all Day:
'Tis Gelladon, to whom our Vows belong,
And Celladon the Subject of our Song.
For whom the Nymphs would dress, the Swains rejoice,
The praise of these, of those the choice;
And if our Joyes were rais'd to this Excess,
Our Pleasures by thy presence made so great:
Some pittying God help thee to guess,
(What fancy cannot well Express.)
Our Languishments by thy Retreat;
Pitty our Swaines, pitty our Virgins more,
And let that pitty haste thee to our shore;
And whilst on happy distant Coasts you are,
Afford us all your sighs, and Cesar all your care.

On a Juniper-Tree, Cut Down to Make Busks.

Whilst happy I Triumphant stood,
The Pride and Glory of the Wood;
My Aromatick Boughs and Fruit,
Did with all other Trees dispute.
Had right by Nature to excel,
In pleasing both the tast and smell:
But to the touch I must confess,
Bore an Ungrateful Sullenness.
My Wealth, like bashful Virgins, I
Yielded with some Reluctancy;
For which my vallue should be more,
Not giving easily my store.
My verdant Branches all the year
Did an Eternal Beauty wear;
Did ever young and gay appear.
Nor needed any tribute pay,

For bounties from the God of Day:
Nor do I hold Supremacy,
(In all the Wood) o'er every Tree.
But even those too of my own Race,
That grow not in this happy place.
But that in which I glory most,
And do my self with Reason boast,
Beneath my shade the other day,
Young Philocles and Claris lay,
Upon my Root she lean'd her head,
And where I grew, he made their Bed:
Whilst I the Canopy more largely spread.
Their trembling Limbs did gently press,
The kind supporting yielding Grass:
Ne'er half so blest as now, to bear
A Swain so Young, a Nimph so fair:
My Grateful Shade I kindly lent,
And every aiding Bough I bent.
So low, as sometimes had the blisse,
To rob the Shepherd of a kiss,
Whilst he in Pleasures far above
The Sence of that degree of Love:
Permitted every stealth I made,
Unjealous of his Rival Shade.
I saw 'em kindle to desire,
Whilst with soft sighs they blew the fire;
Saw the approaches of their joy,
He growing more fierce, and she less Coy,
Saw how they mingled melting Rays,
Exchanging Love a thousand ways.
Kind was the force on every side,
Her new desire she could not hide:
Nor wou'd the Shepherd be deny'd.
Impatient he waits no consent
But what she gave by Languishment,
The blessed Minute he pursu'd;
And now transported in his Arms,
Yeilds to the Conqueror all her Charmes,
His panting Breast, to hers now join'd,
They feast on Raptures unconfin'd;
Vast and Luxuriant, such as prove
The Immortality of Love.
For who but a Divinitie,
Could mingle Souls to that Degree;
And melt 'em into Extasie?
Now like the Phenix, both Expire,
While from the Ashes of their Fire,
Sprung up a new, and soft desire.
Like Charmers, thrice they did invoke,
The God! and thrice new vigor took.
Nor had the Mysterie ended there,

But Claris reassum'd her fear,
And chid the Swain, for having prest,
What she alas wou'd not resist:
Whilst he in whom Loves sacred flame,
Before and after was the same,
Fondly implor'd she wou'd forget
A fault, which he wou'd yet repeat.
From Active Joyes with some they hast,
To a Reflexion on the past;
A thousand times my Covert bless,
That did secure their Happiness:
Their Gratitude to every Tree
They pay, but most to happy me;
The Shepherdess my Bark carest,
Whilst he my Root, Love's Pillow, kist;
And did with sighs, their Fate deplore,
Since I must shelter them no more;
And if before my Joyes were such,
In having heard, and seen too much,
My Grief must be as great and high,
When all abandon'd I shall be,
Doom'd to a silent Destinie.
No more the Charming strife to hear,
The Shepherds Vows, the Virgins fear:
No more a joyful looker on,
Whilst Loves soft Battel's lost and won.
With grief I bow'd my murmering Head,
And all my Christal Dew I shed.
Which did in Claris Pity move,
(Claris whose Soul is made of Love;)
She cut me down, and did translate,
My being to a happier state.
No Martyr for Religion di'd
With half that Unconsidering Pride;
My top was on that Altar laid,
Where Love his softest Offerings paid:
And was as fragrant Incense burn'd,
My body into Busks was turn'd:
Where I still guard the Sacred Store,
And of Loves Temple keep the Door.

On the Death of Mr. Grinhil, the Famous Painter.

I.
What doleful crys are these that fright my sence,
Sad as the Groans of dying Innocence?
The killing Accents now more near Aproach,
And the Infectious Sound,
Spreads and Inlarges all around;

And does all Hearts with Grief and Wonder touch.
The famous Grinhil dead! even he,
That cou'd to us give Immortalitie;
Is to the Eternal silent Groves withdrawn,
Those sullen Groves of Everlasting, Dawn;
Youthful as Flowers, scarce blown, whose opening Leaves,
A wond'rous and a fragrant Prospect gives,
Of what it's Elder Beauties wou'd display,
When they should flourish up to ripning May.
Witty as Poets, warm'd with Love and Wine,
Yet still spar'd Heaven and his Friend,
For both to him were Sacred and Divine:
Nor could he this no more then that offend.
Fixt as a Martyr where he friendship paid,
And Generous as a God,
Distributing his Bounties all abroad;
And soft and gentle as a Love-sick Maid.

II.
Great Master of the Noblest Mysterie,
That ever happy Knowledge did inspire;
Sacred as that of Poetry,
And which the wond'ring World does equally admire.
Great Natures work we do contemn,
When on his Glorious Births we meditate:
The Face and Eies, more Darts received from him,
Then all the Charms she can create.
The Difference is, his Beauties do beget
In the inamour'd Soul a Vertuous Heat:
While Natures Grosser Pieces move,
In the course road of Common Love:
So bold, yet soft, his touches were;
So round each part's so sweet and fair.
That as his Pencil mov'd men thought it prest,
The Lively imitating rising Breast,
Which yield like Clouds, where little Angels rest:
The Limbs all easy as his Temper was;
Strong as his Mind, and manly too;
Large as his Soul his fancy was, and new:
And from himself he copyed every Grace,
For he had all that cou'd adorn a Face,
All that cou'd either Sex subdue.

III.
Each Excellence he had that Youth has in its Pride,
And all Experienced Age cou'd teach,
At once the vigorous fire of this,
And every vertue which that cou'd Express.
In all the heights that both could reach;
And yet alas, in this Perfection di'd.
Dropt like a Blossom with the Northern blest,

(When all the scattered Leaves abroad were cast;)
As quick as if his fate had been in hast:
So have I seen an unfixt Star,
Out-shine the rest of all the Numerous Train,
As bright as that which Guides the Marriner,
Dart swiftly from its darken'd Sphere:
And nere shall sight the World again.

IV.
Ah why shou'd so much knowledge die!
Or with his last kind breath,
Why cou'd he not to some one friend bequeath
The Mighty Legacie!
But 'twas a knowledge given to him alone,
That his eternis'd Name might be
Admir'd to all Posteritie,
By all to whom his grateful Name was known.
Come all ye softer Beauties, come;
Bring Wreaths of Flowers to deck his tomb;
Mixt with the dismal Cypress and the Yew,
For he still gave your Charmes their due:
And from the injuries of Age and Time,
Preserv'd the sweetness of your Prime:
And best knew how t' adore that Sweetness too;
Bring all your Mournful Tributes here,
And let your Eyes a silent sorrow wear,
Till every Virgin for a while become
Sad as his Fate, and like his Picture's Dumb.

A Ballad on Mr. J. H. to Amoret, Asking Why I Was So Sad.

My Amoret, since you must know,
The Grief you say my Eyes do show:
Survey my Heart, where you shall find,
More Love then for your self confin'd.
And though you chide, you'l Pity too,
A Passion which even Rivals you.

Amyntas on a Holy-day
As fine as any Lord of May,
Amongst the Nimphs, and jolly Swaines,
That feed their Flocks upon the Plaines:
Met in a Grove beneath whose shade,
A Match of Dancing they had made.

His Cassock was of Green, as trim
As Grass upon a River brim;
Untoucht or sullied with a spot,
Unprest by either Lamb or Goat:

And with the Air it loosely play'd,
With every motion that he made.

His Sleeves a-many Ribbons ties,
Where one might read Love-Mysteries:
As if that way he wou'd impart,
To all, the Sentiments of his Heart,
Whose Passions by those Colours known,
He with a Charming Pride wou'd own.

His Bonnet with the same was Ti'd,
A Silver Scrip hung by his Side:
His Buskins garnisht A-la-mode,
Were grac'd by every step he Trod;
Like Pan, a Majesty he took,
And like Apollo when he spoke.

His Hook a Wreath of Flowers Braid,
The Present of some Love-sick Maid,
Who all the morning had bestow'd,
And to her Fancy now composed:
Which fresher seem'd when near that place,
To whom the Giver Captive was.

His Eyes their best Attracts put on,
Designing some should be undone;
For he could at his pleasure move,
The Nymphs he lik'd to fall in Love:
Yet so he order'd every Glance,
That still they seem'd but Wounds of Chance.

He well cou'd feign an Innocence,
And taught his Silence Eloquence;
Each Smile he us'd, had got the force,
To Conquer more than soft Discourse:
Which when it serv'd his Ends he'd use,
And subtilly thro' a heart infuse.

His Wit was such it cou'd controul
The Resolutions of a Soul;
That a Religious Vow had made,
By Love it nere wou'd be betra'd:
For when he spoke he well cou'd prove
Their Errors who dispute with Love.

With all these Charms he did Address
Himself to every Shepherdess:
Until the Bag-pipes which did play,
Began the Bus'ness of the day;
And in the taking forth to Dance,
The Lovely Swain became my Chance.

To whom much Passion he did Vow,
And much his Eyes and Sighs did show;
And both imploy'd with so much Art,
I strove in vain to guard my Heart;
And ere the Night our Revels crost,
I was intirely won and lost.

Let me advise thee, Amoret^
Fly from the Baits that he has set
In every grace; which will betray
All Beauties that but look that way:
But thou hast Charms that will secure
A Captive in this Conquerour.

Our Cabal.

Come, my fair Cloris, come away,
Hast thou forgot 'tis Holyday?
And lovely Silvia too make haste,
The Sun is up, the day does waste:
Do'st thou not hear the Musick loud,
Mix'd with the murmur of the Crowd?
How can thy active Feet be still,
And hear the Bagpipes chearful Trill?

Mr. V. U.

Urania's drest as fine and gay,
As if she meant t' out-shine the day;
Or certain that no Victories
Were to be gain'd but by her Eyes;
Her Garment's white, her Garniture
The springing Beauties of the Year,
Which are in such nice Order plac'd,
That Nature is by Art disgrac'd:
Her natural Curling Ebon Hair,
Does loosly wanton in the Air.

Mr. G. V.

With her the young Alexis came,
Whose Eyes dare only speak his Flame:
Charming he is, as fair can be,
Charming without Effeminacy;

Only his Eyes are languishing,
Caus'd by the Pain he feels within;
Yet thou wilt say that Languishment
Is a peculiar Ornament.
Deck'd up he is with Pride and Care,
All Rich and Gay, to please his Fair:
The Price of Flocks h' has made a Prey
To th' Usual Vanity of this day.

My Dear Brother J. C.

After them Damon Piping came,
Who laughs at Cupid and his Flame;
Swears, if the Boy should him approach,
He'd burn his Wings with his own Torch:
But he's too young for Love t' invade,
Though for him languish many a Maid.
His lovely Ayr, his chearful Face,
Adorn'd with many a Youthful Grace,
Beget more Sighs then if with Arts
He should design to conquer Hearts:
The Swains as well as Nymphs submit
To's Charms of Beauty and of Wit.
He'll sing, he'll dance, he'll pipe and play,
And wanton out a Summer's day;
And wheresoever Damon be,
He's still the Soul o'th' Companie.

My Dear Amoret, Mrs. B.

Next Amoret, the true Delight
Of all that do approach her sight:
The Sun in all its Course ne'er met
Ought Fair or Sweet like Amoret.
Alone she came, her Eyes declin'd,
In which you'l read her troubled Mind;
Yes, Silvia y for she'l not deny
She loves, as well as thou and I.
'Tis Philocles, that Proud Ingrate,
That pays her Passion back with Hate;
Whilst she does all but him despise,
And clouds the lustre of her Eyes:
But once to her he did address,
And dying Passion too express;
But soon the Amorous Heat was laid,
He soon forgot the Vows he'd made;
Whilst she in every Silent Grove,

Bewails her easie Faith and Love.
Numbers of Swains do her adore,
But she has vow'd to love no more.

Mr. J. B.

Next Jolly Thirsts came along,
With many Beauties in a Throng.

Mr. Je. B.

With whom the young Amyntas came,
The Author of my Sighs and Flame:
For I'll confess that Truth to you,
Which every Look of mine can show.
Ah how unlike the rest he appears!
With Majesty above his years!
His Eyes so much of Sweetness dress,
Such Wit) such Vigour too express;
That 'twou'd a wonder be to say,
I've seen the Youth, and brought my Heart away.
Ah Claris! Thou that never wert
In danger yet to lose a Heart,
Guard it severely now, for he
Will startle all thy Constancy:
For if by chance thou do'st escape
Unwounded by his Lovely Shape,
Tempt not thy Ruine, lest his Eyes
Joyn with his Tongue to win the Prize:
Such Softness in his Language dwells,
And Tales of Love so well he tells,
Should'st thou attend their Harmony,
Thou'dst be Undone, as well as I;
For sure no Nymph was ever free,
That could Amyntas hear and see.

Mr. N. R. V.

With him the lovely Philocless,
His Beauty heightned by his Dress,
If any thing can add a Grace
To such a Shape, and such a Face,
Whose Natural Ornaments impart
Enough without the help of Art.
His Shoulders cover'd with a Hair,

The Sun-Beams are not half so fair;
Of which the Virgins Bracelets make,
And where for Philocless's sake:
His Beauty such, that one would swear
His face did never take the Air.
On's Cheeks the blushing Roses show,
The rest like whitest Daisies grow:
His Lips, no Berries of the Field,
Nor Cherries, such a Red do yield.
His Eyes all Love, Softening Smile;
And when he speaks, he sighs the while:
His Bashful Grace, with Blushes too,
Gains more then Confidence can do.
With all these Charms he does invade
The Heart, which when he has betray'd,
He slights the Trophies he has won,
And weeps for those he has Undone;
As if he never did intend
His Charms for so severe an End.
And all poor Amoret can gain,
Is pitty from the Lovely Swain:
And if Inconstancy can seem
Agreeable, 'tis so in him.
And when he meets Reproach for it,
He does excuse it with his Wit.

Mr. E. B. and Mrs. F. M.

Next hand in hand the smiling Pair,
Martillo, and the Lovely Fair:
A Bright-Ey'd Phillis, who they say,
Ne'er knew what Love was till to day:
Long has the Gen'rous Youth in vain
Implor'd some Pity for his Pain.
Early abroad he would be seen,
To wait her coming on the Green,
To be the first that t' her should pay
The Tribute of the New-born Day;
Presents her Bracelets with their Names,
And Hooks carv'd out with Hearts and Flames.
And when a stragling Lamb he saw,
And she not by to give it Law,
The pretty Fugitive he'd deck
With Wreaths of Flowers around its Neck;
And gave her ev'ry mark of Love,
Before he could her Pity move.
But now the Youth no more appears
Clouded with Jealousies and Fears:
Nor yet dares Phi His softer Brow

Wear Unconcern, or Coldness now;
But makes him just and kind Returns;
And as He does, so now She burns.

Mr. J. H.

Next Lysidas, that haughty Swain,
With many Beauties in a Train,
All sighing for the Swain, whilst he
Barely returns Civility.
Yet once to each much Love he Vowd,
And strange Fantastique Passion show'd.
Poor Doris, and Luanda too,
And many more whom thou dost know,
Who had not power his Charms to shun,
Too late do find themselves Undone.
His Eyes are Black, and do transcend
All Fancy e'er can comprehend;
And yet no Softness in 'em move.
They kill with Fierceness, not with Love:
Yet he can dress 'em when he list,
With Sweetness none can e'er resist.
His Tongue no Amorous Parley makes,
But with his Looks alone he speaks.
And though he languish yet he'l hide,
That grateful knowledge with his Pride;
And thinks his Liberty is lost,
Not in the Conquest, but the Boast.
Nor will but Love enough impart,
To gain and to secure a heart:
Of which no sooner he is sure,
And that its Wounds are past all Cure.
But for New Victories he prepares,
And leaves the Old to its Despairs:
Success his Boldness does renew,
And Boldness helps him Conquer too,
He having gain'd more hearts than all
Th' rest of the Pastoral Cabal.

Mr. Ed. Bed.

With him Philander, who nere paid
A Sigh or Tear to any Maid:
So innocent and young he is,
He cannot guess what Passion is.
But all the Love he ever knew,
On Lycidas he does bestow:

Who pays his Tenderness again,
Too Amorous for a Swain to a Swain.
A softer Youth was never seen,
His Beauty Maid; but Man, his Mein:
And much more gay than all the rest;
And but Alexis finest Dress'd.
His Eyes towards Lycidas still turn,
As sympathising Flowers to the Sun;
Whilst Lycidas whose Eyes dispense
No less a grateful Influence,
Improves his Beauty, which still fresher grows
Who would not under two such Suns as those?
Cloris you sigh, what Amorous grown?
Pan grant you keep your heart a home:
For I have often heard you Vow,
If any cou'd your heart subdue,
Though Lycidas you nere had seen,
It must be him, or one like him:
Alas I cannot yet forget,
How we have with Amyntas sat
Beneath the Boughs for Summer made,
Our heated Flocks and Us to shade;
Where thou wou'dst wond'rous Stories tell,
Of this Agreeable Infidel.
By what Devices, Charms and Arts,
He us'd to gain and keep his Hearts:
And whilst his Falsehood we won* d Blame,
Thou woud'st commend and praise the same.
And did no greater pleasure take,
Then when of Lycidas we spake;
By this and many Sighs we know,
Thou'rt sensible of Loving too.
Come Chris, come along with us,
And try thy power with Lycidas;
See if that Vertue which you prize,
Be proof against those Conquering Eyes.
That Heart that can no Love admit,
Will hardly stand his shock of Wit;
Come deck thee then in all that's fine,
Perhaps the Conquest may be thine;
They all attend, let's hast to do,
What Love and Musick calls us to.

SONG. The Willing Mistriss.

Amyntas led me to a Grove,
Where all the Trees did shade us;
The Sun it self, though it had Strove,
It could not have betray'd us:

The place secur'd from humane Eyes,
No other fear allows,
But when the Winds that gently rise,
Doe Kiss the yeilding Boughs.
Down there we satt upon the Moss,
And did begin to play
A Thousand Amorous Tricks, to pass
The heat of all the day.
A many Kisses he did give:
And I returned the same
Which made me willing to receive
That which I dare not name.
His Charming Eyes no Aid required
To tell their softning Tale;
On her that was already fir'd,
'Twas Easy to prevaile.
He did but Kiss and Clasp me round,
Whilst those his thoughts Exprest:
And lay'd me gently on the Ground;
Ah who can guess the rest?

SONG. Love Arm'd.

Love in Fantastique Triumph satt,
Whilst Bleeding Hearts a round him flow'd,
For whom Fresh paines he did Create,
And strange Tryanick power he show'd;
From thy Bright Eyes he took his fire,
Which round about, in sport he hurl'd;
But 'twas from mine he took desire,
Enough to undo the Amorous World.

From me he took his sighs and tears,
From thee his Pride and Crueltie;
From me his Languish ments and Feares,
And every Killing Dart from thee;
Thus thou and I, the God have arm'd,
And sett him up a Deity;
But my poor Heart alone is harm'd,
Whilst thine the Victor is, and free.

SONG. The Complaint.

Amyntas that true hearted Swaine,
Upon a Rivers Banck was lay'd,
Where to the Pittying streames he did Complaine
On Silvia that false Charming Maid

While shee was still regardless of his paine.
Ah! Charming Si/via, would he cry;
And what he said, the Echoes wou'd reply:
Be kind or else I dy: Ech: - I dy.
Be kind or else I dy: Ech: - I dy.

Those smiles and Kisses which you give,
Remember Silvia are my due;
And all the Joyes my Rivall does receive,
He ravishes from me not you:

Ah Silvia! can I live and this believe?
Insensibles are toucht to see
My Languishments, and seem to pitty me:
Which I demand of thee: Ech: - of thee.
Which I demand of thee: Ech: - of thee.

Set by Mr. Banister.

SONG. The Invitation.

Damon I cannot blame your will,
'Twas Chance and not Design did kill;
For whilst you did prepare your Charmes,
On purpose Silvia to subdue:
I met the Arrows as they flew,
And sav'd her from their harms.

Alas she cannot make returnes,
Who for a Swaine already Burnes;
A Shepherd whom she does Caress:
With all the softest marks of Love,
And 'tis in vaine thou seek'st to move
The cruel Shepherdess.

Content thee with this Victory,
Think me as faire and young as she:
I'le make thee Garlands all the day,
And in the Groves we'l sit and sing;
Fie Crown thee with the pride o'th' Spring,
When thou art Lord of May.

SONG.

When Jemmy first began to Love,
He was the Gayest Swaine
That ever yet a Flock had drove,

Or danc't upon the Plaine.
T'was then that I, weys me poor Heart,
My Freedom threw away;
And finding sweets in every smart,
I cou'd not say him nay.

And ever when he talkt of Love,
He wou'd his Eyes decline;
And every sigh a Heart would move,
Gued Faith and why not mine?
He'd press my hand, and Kiss it oft,
In silence spoke his Flame.
And whilst he treated me thus soft,
I wisht him more to Blame.

Sometimes to feed my Flocks with him,
My Jemmy wou'd invite me:
Where he the Gayest Songs wou'd sing,
On purpose to delight me.
And Jemmy every Grace displayd,
Which were enough I trow,
To Conquer any Princely Maid,
So did he me I Vow.

But now for Jemmy must I mourn,
Who to the Warrs must go;
His Sheephook to a Sword must turne:
Alack what shall I do?
His Bag-pipe into War-like Sounds,
Must now Exchanged bee:
Instead of Braceletts, fearful Wounds;
Then what becomes of me?

To Mr. Creech (Under the Name of Daphnis) on His Excellent Translation of Lucretius.

Thou great Young Man! Permit amongst the Crowd
Of those that sing thy mighty Praises lowd,
My humble Muse to bring its Tribute too.
Inspir'd by thy vast flight of Verse,
Methinks I should some wondrous thing rehearse,
Worthy Divine Lucretius and Diviner Thou.
But I of Feebler Seeds design'd,
Whilst the slow moving Atomes strove,
With careless heed to form my Mind:
Compos'd it all of Softer Love.
In gentle Numbers all my Songs are Drest,
And when I would thy Glories sing,
What in strong manly Verse I would express,
Turns all to Womannish Tenderness within,

Whilst that which Admiration does inspire,
In other Souls, kindles in mine a Fire.
Let them admire thee on Whilst I this newer way
Pay thee yet more than they:
For more I owe, since thou hast taught me more,
Then all the mighty Bards that went before.
Others long since have Pal'd the vast delight;
In duller Greek and Latin satisfy'd the Appetite
But I unlearn'd in Schools, disdain that mine
Should treated be at any Feast but thine.
Till now, I curst my Birth, my Education,
And more the scanted Customes of the Nation:
Permitting not the Female Sex to tread,
The mighty Paths of Learned Heroes dead.
The God-like Virgil, and great Homers Verse,
Like Divine Mysteries are conceal'd from us.
We are forbid all grateful Theams,
No ravishing thoughts approach our Ear,
The Fulsom Gingle of the times,
Is all we are allow'd to understand or hear.
But as of old, when men unthinking lay,
Ere Gods were worshipt, or ere Laws were fram'd
The wiser Bard that taught 'em first t' obey,
Was next to what he taught, ador'd and fam'd;
Gentler they grew, their words and manners chang'd,
And salvage now no more the Woods they rang'd.
So thou by this Translation dost advance
Our Knowledg from the State of Ignorance,
And equals us to Man! Ah how can we,
Enough Adore, or Sacrifice enough to thee.

The Mystick Terms of Rough Philosophy,
Thou dost so plain and easily express;
Yet Deck'st them in so soft and gay a Dress:
So intelligent to each Capacity,
That they at once Instruct and Charm the Sense,
With heights of Fancy, heights of Eloquence:
And Reason over all Unfettered plays,
Wanton and undisturb'd as Summers Breeze;
That gliding murmurs o're the Trees:
And no hard Notion meets or stops its way
It Pierces, Conquers and Compels,
Beyond poor Feeble Faith's dull Oracles.
Faith the despairing Souls content,
Faith the Last Shift of Routed Argument.

Hail Sacred Wadham I whom the Muses Grace
And from the Rest of all the Reverend Pile,
Of Noble Pallaces, design'd thy Space:
Where they in soft retreat might dwell.
They blest thy Fabrick, and said Do thou,

Our Darling Sons contain;
We thee our Sacred Nursery Ordain,
They said and blest, and it was so.
And if of old the Fanes of Silvian Gods,
Were worshipt as Divine Aboads;
If Courts are held as Sacred Things,
For being the Awful Seats of Kings.
What Veneration should be paid,
To thee that hast such wondrous Poets made.
To Gods for fear, Devotion was design'd,
And Safety made us bow to Majesty;
Poets by Nature Aw and Charm the Mind,
Are born not made by dull Religion or Necessity.

The Learned Thirsts did to thee belong,
Who Athens Plague has so divinely Sung.
Thirsis to wit, as sacred friendship true,
Paid Mighty Cowley's Memory its due.
Thirsts who whilst a greater Plague did reign,
Then that which Athens did Depopulate:
Scattering Rebellious Fury o're the Plain,
That threaten'd Ruine to the Church and State,
Unmov'd he stood, and fear'd no Threats of Fate.
That Loyal Champion for the Church and Crown,
That Noble Ornament of the Sacred Gown,
Still did his Soveraign's Cause Espouse,
And was above the Thanks of the mad Senate-house.
Strephon the Great, whom last you sent abroad,
Who Writ, and Lov'd, and Lookt like any God;
For whom the Muses mourn, the Love-sick Maids
Are Languishing in Melancholly Shades.
The Cupids flag their Wings, their Bows untie,
And useless Quivers hang neglected by,
And scatter'd Arrows all around 'em lye.
By murmuring Brooks the careless Deities are laid,
Weeping their rifled power now Noble Strephon' s Dead.

Ah Sacred Wadham! should'st thou never own
But this delight of all Mankind and thine;
For Ages past of Dulness, this alone,
This Charming Hero would Attone.
And make thee Glorious to succeeding time;
But thou like Natures self disdain'st to be,
Stinted to Singularity.
Even as fast as she thou dost produce,
And over all the Sacred Mystery infuse.
No sooner was fam'd Strfphort's Glory set,
Strephon the Soft, the Lovely and the Great;
But Daphnis rises like the Morning-Star,
That guides the Wandring Traveller from afar.
Daphnis whom every Grace, and Muse inspires,

Scarce Strephons Ravishing Poetic Fires
So kindly warm, or so divinely Cheer.
Advance Young Daphnis, as thou hast begun,
So let thy Mighty Race be run.
Thou in thy large Poetick Chace,
Begin'st where others end the Race.
If now thy Grateful Numbers are so strong,
If they so early can such Graces show,
Like Beauty so surprizing, when so Young,
What Daphnis will thy Riper Judgment do,
When thy Unbounded Verse in their own Streams shall flow!
What Wonder will they not produce,
When thy Immortal Fancy's loose;
Unfetter'd, Unconfin'd by any other Muse!
Advance Young Daphnis then, and mayst thou prove
Still sacred in thy Poetry and Love.
May all the Groves with Daphnis Songs be blest,
Whilst every Bark is with thy Disticks drest.
May Timerous Maids learn how to Love from thence
And the Glad Shepherd Arts of Eloquence.
And when to Solitude thou would'st Retreat,
May their tun'd Pipes thy Welcome celebrate.
And all the Nymphs strow Garlands at thy Feet.
May all the Purling Streams that murmuring pass,
The Shady Groves and Banks of Flowers,
The kind reposing Beds of Grass,
Contribute to their Softer Hours.
Mayst thou thy Muse and Mistress there Caress,
And may one heighten to 'thers Happiness.
And whilst thou so divinely dost Converse,
We are content to know and to admire thee in thy Sacred Verse.

To Mrs. W. On Her Excellent Verses (Writ in Praise of Some I Had Made on the Earl of Rochester) Written In a Fit of Sickness.

Enough kind Heaven! to purpose I have liv'd,
And all my Sighs and Languishments surviv'd.
My Stars in vain their sullen influence have shed,
Round my till now Unlucky Head:
I pardon all the Silent Hours I've griev'd,
My Weary Nights, and Melancholy Days;
When no Kind Power my Pain Reliev'd,
I lose you all, ye sad Remembrancers,
I lose you all in New-born Joys,
Joys that will dissipate my Falling Tears.
The Mighty Soul of Rochester's reviv'd,
Enough Kind Heaven to purpose I have liv'd.
I saw the Lovely Phantom, no Disguise,
Veil'd the blest Vision from my Eyes,

'Twas all o're Rochester that pleas'd and did surprize.
Sad as the Grave I sat by Glimmering Light,
Such as attends Departing Souls by Night.
Pensive as absent Lovers left alone,
Or my poor Dove, when his Fond Mate was gone.
Silent as Groves when only Whispering Gales,
Sigh through the Rushing Leaves,
As softly as a Bashful Shepherd Breaths,
To his Lov'd Nymph his Amorous Tales.
So dull I was, scarce Thought a Subject found,
Dull as the Light that gloom'd around;
When lo the Mighty Spirit appear'd,
All Gay, all Charming to my sight;
My Drooping Soul it Rais'd and Cheer'd,
And cast about a Dazling Light.
In every part there did appear,
The Great, the God-like Rochester,
His Softness all, his Sweetness everywhere.
It did advance, and with a Generous Look,
To me Addrest, to worthless me it spoke:
With the same wonted Grace my Muse it prais'd,'
With the same Goodness did my Faults Correct;
And careful of the Fame himself first rais'd,
Obligingly it School'd my loose Neglect.
The soft, the moving Accents soon I knew
The gentle Voice made up of Harmony;
Through the Known Paths of my glad Soul it flew;
I knew it straight, it could no others be,
'Twas not Alied but very very he.
So the All-Ravisht Swain that hears
The wondrous Musick of the Sphears,
For ever does the grateful Sound retain,
Whilst all his Oaten Pipes and Reeds,
The Rural Musick of the Groves and Meads,
Strive to divert him from the Heavenly Song in vain.
He hates their harsh and Untun'd Lays,
Which now no more his Soul and Fancy raise.
But if one Note of the remembred Air
He chance again to hear,
He starts, and in a transport cries, 'Tis there.
He knows it all by that one little taste,
And by that grateful Hint remembers all the rest.
Great, Good, and Excellent, by what new way
Shall I my humble Tribute pay,
For this vast Glory you my Muse have done,
For this great Condescension shown!
So Gods of old sometimes laid by
Their Awful Trains of Majesty,
And chang'd ev'n Heav'n a while for Groves and Plains,
And to their Fellow-Gods preferr'd the lowly Swains,
And Beds of Flow'rs would oft compare

To those of Downey Clouds, or yielding Air;
At purling Streams would drink in homely Shells,
Put offthe God, to Revel it in Woods and Shepherds Cells;
Would listen to their Rustick Songs, and show
Such Divine Goodness in Commending too,
Whilst the transported Swain the Honour pays
With humble Adoration, humble Praise.

The Sence of a Letter Sent Me, Made into Verse; To a New Tune.

I.
In vain I have labour'd the Victor to prove
Of a Heart that can ne'er give Admittance to Love:
So hard to be won
That nothing so young
Could e'er have resisted a Passion so long.

II.
But nothing I left unattempted or said,
To soften the Heart of the Pityless Maid;
Yet still she was shy,
And would blushing deny,
Whilst her willinger Eyes gave her Language the Lye.

III.
When before the Impregnable Fort I lay down,
I resolv'd or to die, or to Purchase Renown,
But how vain was the Boast!
All the Glory I lost,
And now vanquish'd and sham'd I've quitted my Post.

The Return.

I.
Amyntas, whilst you
Have an Art to subdue,
And can conquer a Heart with a Look or a Smile;
You Pityless grow,
And no Faith will allow;
'Tis the Glory you seek when you rifle the Spoil.

II.
Your soft warring Eyes,
When prepar'd for the Prize,
Can laugh at the Aids of my feeble Disdain;
You can humble the Foe,
And soon make her to know

Tho' she arms her with Pride, her Efforts are but vain.

III.
But Shepherd beware,
Though a Victor you are;
A Tyrant was never secure in his Throne;
Whilst proudly you aim
New Conquests to gain,
Some hard-hearted Nymph may return you your own.

On a Copy of Verses made in a Dream and Sent to Me in a Morning Before I was Awake.

Amyntas, if your Wit in Dreams
Can furnish you with Theams,
What must it do when your Soul looks abroad,
Quick'nd with Agitations of the Sence,
And dispossest of Sleeps dull heavy Load,
When ev'ry Syllable has Eloquence?
And if by Chance such Wounds you make,
And in your Sleep such welcome Mischiefs do;
What are your Pow'rs when you're awake,
Directed by Design and Reason too?
I slept, as duller Mortals use,
Without the Musick of a Thought,
When by a gentle Breath, soft as thy Muse,
Thy Name to my glad Ear was brought:
Amyntas! cry'd the Page And at the Sound,
My list'ning Soul unusual Pleasure found.
So the Harmonius Spheres surprize,
Whilst the All-Ravish'd Shepherd gazes round,
And wonders whence the Charms should rise,
That can at once both please and wound.
Whilst trembling I unript the Seal
Of what you'd sent,
My Heart with an Impatient Zeal,
Without my Eyes, would needs reveal
Its Bus'ness and Intent.

But so beyond the Sence they were
Of ev'ry scribling Lovers common Art,
That now I find an equal share
Of Love and Admiration in my Heart.
And while I read, in vain I strove
To hide the Pleasure which I took;
Bellario saw in ev'ry Look
My smiling Joy and blushing Love.
Soft ev'ry word, easie each Line, and true;
Brisk, witty, manly, strong and gay;
The Thoughts are tender all, and new,

And Fancy ev'ry where does gently play,
Amyntas, if you thus go on,
Like an unwearied Conqueror day and night,
The World at last must be undone.
You do not only kill at sight,
But like a Parthian in your flight,
Whether you Rally or Retreat,
You still have Arrows for Defeat.

To My Lady Morland at Tunbridge.

As when a Conqu'rour does in Triumph come
And proudly leads the vanquish'd Captives home,
The Joyful People croud in ev'ry Street,
And with loud shouts of Praise the Victor greet;
While some whom Chance or Fortune kept away,
Desire at least the Story of the Day;
How brave the Prince, how gay the Chariot was,
How beautiful he look'd, with what a Grace;
Whether upon his Head he Plumes did wear;
Or if a Wreath of Bays adorn'd his Hair:
They hear 'tis wondrous fine, and long much more
To see the Hero then they did before.
So when the Marvels by Report I knew,
Of how much Beauty, Claris, dwelt in you;
How many Slaves your Conquering Eyes had won,
And how the gazing Crowd admiring throng:
I wish'd to see, and much a Lover grew
Of so much Beauty, though my Rivals too.
I came and saw, and blest my Destiny;
I found it Just you should out-Rival me.
'Twas at the Altar, where more Hearts were giv'n
To you that day, then were address'd to Heav'n.
The Rev'rend Man whose Age and Mystery
Had rendred Youth and Beauty Vanity,
By fatal Chance casting his Eyes your way,
Mistook the duller Bus'ness of the Day,
Forgot the Gospel, and began to Pray.
Whilst the Enamour'd Crowd that near you prest,
Receiving Darts which none could e'er resist,
Neglected the Mistake o'th' Love-sick Priest.
Ev'n my Devotion, Claris, you betray'd,
And I to Heaven no other Petition made,
But that you might all other Nymphs out-do
In Cruelty as well as Beauty too.
I call'd Amyntas Faithless Swain before,
But now I find 'tis Just he should Adore.
Not to love you, a wonder sure would be,
Greater then all his Perjuries to me.

And whilst I Blame him, I Excuse him too;
Who would not venture Heav'n to purchase you?
But Charming Cloris, you too meanly prize
The more deserving Glories of your Eyes,
If you permit him on an Amorous score,
To be your Slave, who was my Slave before.
He oft has Fetters worn, and can with ease
Admit 'em or dismiss 'em when he please.
A Virgin-Heart you merit, that ne'er found
It could receive, till from your Eyes, the Wound;
A Heart that nothing but your Force can fear,
And own a Soul as Great as you are Fair.

Song to Ceres.

In the Wavering Nymph, or Mad Amyntas.

I.
Ceres, Great Goddess of the bounteous Year,
Who load'st the Teeming Earth with Gold and Grain,
Blessing the Labours of th' Industrious Swain,
And to their Plaints inclin'st thy gracious Ear:
Behold two fair Chilian Lovers lie
Prostrate before thy Deity;
Imploring thou wilt grant the Just Desires
Of two Chaste Hearts that burn with equal Fires.

II.
Amyntas he, brave, generous and young;
Whom yet no Vice his Youth has e'er betray'd:
And Chaste Urania is the Lovely Maid;
His Daughter who has serv'd thy Altars long,
As thy High Priest: A Dowry he demands
At the young Amorous Shepherds hands:
Say, gentle Goddess, what the Youth must give,
E'er the Bright Maid he can from thee receive.

Song in the Same Play, by the Wavering Nymph.

Pan, grant that I may never prove
So great a Slave to fall in love,
And to an Unknown Deity
Resign my happy Liberty:
I love to see the Amorous Swains
Unto my Scorn their Hearts resign:
With Pride I see the Meads and Plains
Throng'd all with Slaves, and they all mine:

Whilst I the whining Fools despise,
That pay their Homage to my Eyes.

The Disappointment.

I.

One day the Amorous Lysander,
By an impatient Passion sway'd,
Surpriz'd fair Chris, that lov'd Maid,
Who could defend her self no longer.
All things did with his Love conspire;
The gilded Planet of the Day,
In his gay Chariot drawn by Fire,
Was now descending to the Sea,
And left no Light to guide the World,
But what from Cloris Brighter Eyes was hurld.

II.

In a lone Thicket made for Love,
Silent as yielding Maids Consent,
She with a Charming Languishment,
Permits his Force, yet gently strove;
Her Hands his Bosom softly meet,
But not to put him back designed,
Rather to draw 'em on inclin'd:
Whilst he lay trembling at her Feet,
Resistance 'tis in vain to show;
She wants the pow'r to say Ah! What d^ye do?

III.

Her Bright Eyes sweet, and yet severe,
Where Love and Shame confus'dly strive,
Fresh Vigor to Lysander give;
And breathing faintly in his Ear,
She cry'd Cease, Cease your vain Desire,
Or I'll call out What would you do?
My Dearer Honour evn to You
I cannot, must not give Retire,
Or take this Life, whose chiefest part
I gave you with the Conquest of my Heart.

IV.

But he as much unus'd to Fear,
As he was capable of Love,
The blessed minutes to improve,
Kisses her Mouth, her Neck, her Hair;
Each Touch her new Desire Alarms,
His burning trembling Hand he prest
Upon her swelling Snowy Brest,

While she lay panting in his Arms.
All her Unguarded Beauties lie
The Spoils and Trophies of the Enemy.

V.
And now without Respect or Fear,
He seeks the Object of his Vows,
(His Love no Modesty allows)
By swift degrees advancing where
His daring Hand that Altar seiz'd,
Where Gods of Love do sacrifice:
That Awful Throne, that Paradice
Where Rage is calm'd, and Anger pleas'd;
That Fountain where Delight still flows,
And gives the Universal World Repose.

VI.
Her Balmy Lips incountring his,
Their Bodies, as their Souls, are joyn'd;
Where both in Transports Unconfin'd
Extend themselves upon the Moss.
Claris half dead and breathless lay;
Her soft Eyes cast a Humid Light,
Such as divides the Day and Night;
Or falling Stars, whose Fires decay:
And now no signs of Life she shows,
But what in short-breath'd Sighs returns and goes.

VII.
He saw how at her Length she lay;
He saw her rising Bosom bare;
Her loose thin Robes, through which appear
A Shape design'd for Love and Play;
Abandoned by her Pride and Shame.
She does her softest Joys dispence,
OfFring her Virgin-Innocence
A Victim to Loves Sacred Flame;
While the o'er-Ravish'd Shepherd lies
Unable to perform the Sacrifice.

VIII.
Ready to taste a thousand Joys,
The too transported hapless Swain
Found the vast Pleasure turn'd to Pain;
Pleasure which too much Love destroys:
The willing Garments by he laid,
And Heaven all open'd to his view,
Mad to possess, himself he threw
On the Defenceless Lovely Maid.
But Oh what envying God conspires
To snatch his Power, yet leave him the Desire!

IX.

Nature's Support, (without whose Aid
She can no Humane Being give)
It self now wants the Art to live;
Faintness its slack'ned Nerves invade:
In vain th' in raged Youth essay 'd
To call its fleeting Vigor back,
No motion 'twill from Motion take;
Excess of Love his Love betray'd:
In vain he Toils, in vain Commands;
The Insensible fell weeping in his Hand.

X.

In this so Amorous Cruel Strife,
Where Love and Fate were too severe,
The poor Lysander in despair
Renounc'd his Reason with his Life:
Now all the brisk and active Fire
That should the Nobler Part inflame,
Serv'd to increase his Rage and Shame,
And left no Spark for New Desire:
Not all her Naked Charms cou'd move
Or calm that Rage that had debauch'd his Love.

XL

Cloris returning from the Trance
Which Love and soft Desire had bred,
Her timerous Hand she gently laid
(Or guided by Design or Chance)
Upon that Fabulous Priapus,
That Potent God, as Poets feign;
But never did young Shepherdess,
Gath'ring of Fern upon the Plain,
More nimbly draw her Fingers back,
Finding beneath the verdant Leaves a Snake

XII.

Than Cloris her fair Hand withdrew,
Finding that God of her Desires
Disarm'd of all his Awful Fires,
And Cold as Flow'rs bath'd in the Morning Dew.
Who can the Nymph's Confusion guess?
The Blood forsook the hinder Place,
And strew'd with Blushes all her Face,
Which both Disdain and Shame exprest:
And from Ly Sander's Arms she fled,
Leaving him fainting on the Gloomy Bed.

XIII.

Like Lightning through the Grove she hies,

Or Daphne from the Delphick God,
No Print upon the grassey Road
She leaves, t' instruct Pursuing Eyes.
The Wind that wanton'd in her Hair,
And with her Ruffled Garments plaid,
Discover'd in the Flying Maid
All that the Gods e'er made, if Fair.
So Venus, when her Love was slain,
With Fear and Haste flew o'er the Fatal Plain.

XIV.
The Nymph's Resentments none but I
Can well Imagine or Condole:
But none can guess Lysander's Soul,
But those who sway'd his Destiny.
His silent Griefs swell up to Storms,
And not one God his Fury spares;
He curs'd his Birth, his Fate, his Stars;
But more the Shepherdess's Charms,
Whose soft bewitching Influence
Had Damn'd him to the Hell of Impotence.

On a Locket of Hair Wove in a True-Loves Knot, given me by Sir R.O.

What means this Knot, in Mystick Order Ty'd,
And which no Humane Knowledge can divider
Not the Great Conqu'rours Sword can this undo
Whose very Beauty would divert the Blow.
Bright Relique! Shrouded in a Shrine of Gold!
Less Myst'ry made a Deity of Old.
Fair Charmer! Tell me by what pow'rful Spell
You into this Confused Order fell?
If Magick could be wrought on things Divine,
Some Amorous Sybil did thy Form design
In some soft hour, which the Prophetick Maid
In Nobler Mysteries of Love employ'd.
Wrought thee a Hieroglyphick, to express
The wanton God in all his Tenderness;
Thus shaded, and thus all adorn'd with Charms,
Harmless, Unfletch'd, without Offensive Arms,
He us'd of Old in shady Groves to Play,
E'er Swains broke Vows, or Nymphs were vain and coy,
Or Love himself had Wings to fly away.J
Or was it (his Almighty Pow'r to prove)
Design'd a Quiver for the God of Love?
And all these shining Hairs which th'inspir'd Maid
Has with such strange Mysterious Fancy laid,
Are meant his Shafts; the subtlest surest Darts
That ever Conqu'red or Secur'd his Hearts;

Darts that such tender Passions do convey,
Not the young Wounder is more soft than they
'Tis so; the Riddle I at last have learn'd:
But found it when I was too far concerned.

The Dream. A Song.

I.
The Grove was gloomy all around,
Murm'ring the Streams did pass,
Where fond Astrae laid her down
Upon a Bed of Grass.

I slept and saw a piteous sight,
Cupid a weeping lay,
Till both his little Stars of Light
Had wept themselves away.

II.
Methought I ask'd him why he cry'd,
My Pity led me on:
All sighing the sad Boy reply'd,
Alas I am undone!

As I beneath yon Myrtles lay,
Down by Diana's Springs,
Amyntas stole my Bow away,
And Pinion'd both my Wings.

III.
Alas! cry'd I, 'twas then thy Darts
Wherewith he wounded me:
Thou Mighty Deity of Hearts,
He stole his Pow'r from thee.

Revenge thee, if a God thou be,
Upon the Amorous Swain;
I'll set thy Wings at Liberty,
And thou shalt fly again.

IV.
And for this Service on my Part,
All I implore of thee,
Is, That thou't wound Amyntas Heart,
And make him die for me.

His Silken Fetters I Unty'd,
And the gay Wings display'd;
Which gently fann'd, he mounts and cry'd,

Farewel fond easy Maid.

V.
At this I blush'd, and angry grew
I should a God believe;
And waking found my Dream too true,
Alas I was a Slave.

A Letter to a Brother of the Pen in Tribulation.

Poor Damon! Art thou caught? Is't e'vn so?
Art thou become a (a)Tabernacler too?
Where sure thou dost not mean to Preach or Pray,
Unless it be the clean contrary way:
This holy (b) time I little thought thy sin
Deserv'd a Tub to do its Pennance in.
O how you'll for th' Aegyptian Flesh-pots wish,
When you'r half-famish'd with your Lenten-dish,
Your Almonds, Currant, Biskets hard and dry,
Food that will Soul and Body mortifie:
Damn'd Penetential Drink, that will infuse
Dull Principles into thy Grateful Muse.
Pox on't that you must needs be fooling now,
Just when the Wits had greatest(c) need of you.
Was Summer then so long a coming on,
That you must make an Artificial one?
Much good may't do thee; but 'tis thought thy Brain
E'er long will wish for cooler Days again.
For Honesty no more will I engage:
I durst have sworn thou'dst had thy Pusillage.
Thy Looks the whole Cabal have cheated too;
But thou wilt say, most of the Wits do so.
Is this thy writing Plays? (d) who thought thy Wit
An Interlude of Whoring would admit?
To Poetry no more thou'lt be inclin'd,
Unless in Verse to damn all Woman-kind:
And 'tis but Just thou shouldst in Rancor grow
Against that Sex that has Confin'd thee so.
All things in Nature now are Brisk and Gay
At the Approaches of the Blooming May:
The new-fletch'd Birds do in our Arbors sing
A Thousand Airs to welcome in the Spring;
Whilst ev'ry Swain is like a Bridegroom drest,
And ev'ry Nymph as going to a Feast:
The Meadows now their flowry Garments wear,
And ev'ry Grove does in its Pride appear:
Whilst thou poor Damon in close Rooms are pent,
Where hardly thy own Breath can find a vent.
Yet that too is a Heaven, compared to th' Task

Of Codling every Morning in a Cask.
Now I could curse this Female, but I know,
She needs it not, that thus cou'd handle you.
Besides, that Vengeance does to thee belong.
And 'twere Injustice to disarm thy Tongue.
Curse then, dear Swain, that all the Youth may hear,
And from thy dire Mishap be taught to fear.
Curse till thou hast undone the Race, and all
That did contribute to thy Spring and Fall.

(a)So be called a Sweating-Tub.
(b) Lent,
(c) I wanted a Prologue to a Play,
(d) He pretended to Retire to Write.

The Reflection: A Song.

I.
Poor Lost Serena, to Bemoan
The Rigor of her Fate,
High'd to a Rivers-side alone,
Upon whose Brinks she sat.
Her Eyes, as if they would have spar'd,
The Language of her Tongue,
In Silent Tears a while declar'd
The Sense of all her wrong.

II.
But they alas too feeble were,
Her Grief was swoln too high
To be Exprest in Sighs and Tears;
She must or speak or dye.
And thus at last she did complain,
Is this the Faith, said she,
Which thou allowest me, Cruel Swain,
For that I gave to thee?

III.
Heaven knows with how much Innocence
I did my Soul Incline
To thy Soft Charmes of Eloquence,
And gave thee what was mine.
I had not one Reserve in Store,
But at thy Feet I lay'd
Those Arms that Conquer'd heretofore,
Tho' now thy Trophies made.

IV.
Thy Eyes in Silence told their Tale

Of Love in such a way,
That 'twas as easie to Prevail,
As after to Betray.
And when you spoke my Listning Soul,
Was on the Flattery Hung:
And I was lost without Controul,
Such Musick grac'd thy Tongue.

V.

Alas how long in vain you strove
My coldness to divert!
How long besieg'd it round with Love,
Before you won the Heart.
What Arts you us'd, what Presents made,
What Songs, what Letters writ:
And left no Charm that cou'd invade,
Or with your Eyes or Wit.

VI.

Till by such Obligations Prest,
By such dear Perjuries won:
I heedlesly Resign'd the rest,
And quickly was undone.
For as my Kindling Flames increase,
Yours glimeringly decay:
The Rifled Joys no more can Please,
That once oblig'd your Stay.

VII.

Witness ye Springs, ye Meads and Groves,
Who oft were conscious made
To all our Hours and Vows of Love;
Witness how I'm Betray'd.
Trees drop your Leaves, be Gay no more,
Ye Rivers waste and drye:
Whilst on your Melancholy Shore,
I lay me down and dye.

SONG. To Pesibles Tune.

I.

'Twas when the Fields were gay,
The Groves and every Tree:
Just when the God of Day,
Grown weary of his Sway,
Descended to the Sea,
And Gloomy Light around did all the World survey.
'Twas then the Hapless Swain,
Amyntas, to Complain

Of Silvia's cold Disdain,
Retir'd to Silent Shades;
Where by a Rivers Side,
His Tears did swell the Tide,
As he upon the Brink was lay'd.

II.
Ye Gods, he often cry'd,
Why did your Powers design
In Silvia so much Pride,
Such Falshood too beside,
With Beauty so Divine?
Why should so much of Hell with so much Heaven joyn?
Be witness every Shade,
How oft the lovely Maid
Her tender Vows has paid;
Yet with the self-same Breath,
With which so oft before,
And solemnly she swore,
Pronounces now Amyntas Death.

III.
But, Charming Nymph, beware,
Whilst I your Victim die,
Some One, my Perjur'd Fair,
Revenging my Despair,
Will prove as false to thee;
Which yet my wandring Ghost wou'd look more pale to see.
For I shall break my Tomb,
And nightly as I rome,
Shall to my Silvia come,
And show the Piteous Sight;
My bleeding Bosom too,
Which wounds were given by you;
Then vanish in the Shades of Night.

SONG. On her Loving Two Equally.

Set by Captain Pack.

I.
How strongly does my Passion flow,
Divided equally 'twixt two?
Damon had ne'er subdu'd my Heart,
Had not Alexis took his part;
Nor cou'd Alexis pow'rful prove.
Without my Damons Aid, to gain my Love.

II.

When my Alexis present is,
Then I for Damon sigh and mourn;
But when Alexis I do miss,
Damon gains nothing but my Scorn.
But if it chance they both are by,
For both alike I languish, sigh, and die.

III.
Cure then, thou mighty winged God,
This restless Feaver in my Blood;
One Golden-Pointed Dart take back:
But which, O Cupid, wilt thou take?
If Damons, all my Hopes are crost;
Or that of my Alexis, I am lost.

The Counsel. A Song.

Set by Captain Pack.

I.
A Pox upon this needless Scorn:
Sylvia, for shame the Cheat give o'er:
The End to which the Fair are born,
Is not to keep their Charms in store:
But lavishly dispose in haste
Of Joys which none but Youth improve;
Joys which decay when Beauty's past;
And who, when Beauty's past, will love?

II.
When Age those Glories shall deface,
Revenging all your cold Disdain;
And Sylvia shall neglected pass,
By every once-admiring Swain;
And we no more shall Homage pay:
When you in vain too late shall burn,
If Love increase, and Youth decay,
Ah Sylvia! who will make Return?

III.
Then haste, my Sylvia, to the Grove,
Where all the Sweets of May conspire
To teach us ev'ry Art of Love,
And raise our Joys of Pleasure higher:
Where while embracing we shall lie
Loosly in Shades on Beds of Flow'rs,
The duller World while we defie,
Years will be Minutes, Ages Hours.

SONG. 'The Surprize.

Set by Mr. Farmer.

I.
Phillis, whose Heart was Unconfm'd,
And free as Flow'rs on Meads and Plains,
None boasted of her being Kind,
'Mong'st all the languishing and amorous Swains.
No Sighs or Tears the Nymph cou'd move,
To pity or return their Love.

II.
Till on a time the hapless Maid
Retir'd to shun the Heat o'th' Day
Into a Grove, beneath whose shade
Strepbon the careless Shepherd sleeping lay:
But O such Charms the Youth adorn,
Love is reveng'd for all her Scorn.

III.
Her Cheeks with Blushes cover'd were,
And tender Sighs her Bosom warm,
A Softness in her Eyes appear;
Unusual Pain she feels from ev'ry Charm:
To Woods and Ecchoes now she cries,
For Modesty to speak denies.

SONG.

I.
Ah! what can mean that eager Joy
Transports my Heart when you appear?
Ah, Strephon! you my Thoughts imploy
In all that's Charming, all that's Dear.
When you your pleasing Story tell,
A Softness does invade each Part,
And I with Blushes own I feel
Something too tender at my Heart.

II.
At your approach my Blushes rise,
And I at once both wish and fear;
My wounded Soul mounts to my Eyes,
As it would prattle Stories there.
Take, take that Heart that needs must go;
But, Shepherd, see it kindly us'd:

For who such Presents will bestow,
If this, alas! should be abus'd?

The Invitation: A Song. To a New Scotch Tune.

I.
Come, my Phillis let us improve
Both our Joyes of Equal Love:
While we in yonder Shady Grove,
Count Minutes by our Kisses.
See the Flowers how sweetly they spread,
And each Resigns his Gawdy Head,
To make for us a Fragrant Bed,
To practice o'er New Blisses.

II.
The Sun it self with Love does conspire,
And sends abroad his ardent Fire,
And kindly seems to bid us retire,
And shade us from his Glory;
Then come, my Phillls^ do not fear;
All that your Swain desires there,
Is by those Eyes anew to swear
How much he does adore ye.

III.
Phillis, in vain you shed those Tears;
Why do you blush? Oh speak your Fears!
There's none but your Amyntas hears:
What means this pretty Passion?
Can you fear your Favours will cloy
Those that the Blessing does enjoy?
Ah no! such needless Thoughts destroy:
This Nicety's out of Fashion.

IV.
When thou hast done, by Pan I swear,
Thou wilt unto my Eyes appear
A thousand times more Charming and Fair,
Then thou wert to my first Desire:
That Smile was kind, and now thou'rt wise,
To throw away this Coy Disguise,
And by the vigor of thy Eyes,
Declare thy Youth and Fire.

Silvio's Complaint: A Song. To a Fine Scotch Tune.

I.

In the Blooming Time o'th' year,
In the Royal Month of May:
Au the Heaves were glad and clear,
Au the Earth was Fresh and Gay.
A noble Youth but all Forlorn,
Lig'd Sighing by a Spring:
'Twere better I's was nere Born,
Ere wisht to be a King.

II.

Then from his Starry Eyne,
Muckle Showers of Christal Fell:
To bedew the Roses Fine,
That on his Cheeks did dwell.
And ever 'twixt his Sighs he'd cry,
How Bonny a Lad I'd been,
Had I, weys me, nere Aim'd high,
Or wisht to be a King.

III.

With Dying Clowdy Looks,
Au the Fields and Groves he kens:
Au the deeding Murmuring Brooks,
(Noo his Unambitious Friends)
Tol which he eance with Mickle Cheer
His Bleating Flocks woud bring:
And crys, woud God I'd dy'd here,
Ere wisht to be a King.

IV.

How oft in Yonder Mead,
Cover'd ore with Painted Flowers:
Au the Dancing Youth I've led,
Where we past our Blether Hours.
In Yonder Shade, in Yonder Grove,
How Blest the Nymphs have been:
Ere I for Pow'r Debaucht Love,
Or wisht to be a King.

V.

Not add the Arcadian Swains,
In their Pride and Glory Clad:
Not au the Spacious Plains,
Ere coud Boast a Bleether Lad.
When ere I Pip'd, or Danc'd, or Ran,
Or leapt, or whirPd the Sling:
The Flowry Wreaths I still won,
And wisht to be a King.

VI.

But Curst be yon Tall Oak,
And Old Thirsis be accurst:
There I first my peace forsook,
There I learnt Ambition first.
Such Glorious Songs of Hero's Crown'd,
The Restless Swain woud Sing:
My Soul unknown desires found,
And Languisht to be King.

VII.
Ye Garlands, wither now,
Fickle Glories, vanish all:
Ye Wreaths that deckt my Brow,
To the ground neglected fall.
No more my sweet Repose molest,
Nor to my Fancies bring
The Golden Dreams of being Blest
With Titles of a King.

VIII.
Ye Noble Youths, beware,
Shun Ambitious powerful Tales:
Distructive, False, and Fair,
Like the Oceans Flattering Gales.
See how my Youth and Glories lye,
Like Blasted Flowers i'th' Spring:
My Fame, Renown, and all dye,
For wishing to be King.

In Imitation of Horace.

I.
What mean those Amorous Curles of Jet!
For what heart-Ravisht Maid
Dost thou thy Hair in order set,
Thy Wanton Tresses Braid?
And thy vast Store of Beauties open lay,
That the deluded Fancy leads astray.

II.
For pitty hide thy Starry eyes,
Whose Languishments destroy:
And look not on the Slave that dyes
With an Excess of Joy.
Defend thy Coral Lips, thy Amber Breath;
To taste these Sweets lets in a Certain Death.

III.
Forbear, fond Charming Youth, forbear,

Thy words of Melting Love:
Thy Eyes thy Language well may spare,
One Dart enough can move.
And she that hears thy voice and sees thy Eyes
With too much Pleasure, too much Softness dies.

IV.
Cease, Cease, with Sighs to warm my Soul,
Or press me with thy Hand:
Who can the kindling fire controul,
The tender force withstand?
Thy Sighs and Touches like wing'd Lightning fly,
And are the Gods of Loves Artillery.

To Lysander, Who Made Some Verses on a Discourse of Loves Fire.

I.
In vain, dear Youth, you say you love,
And yet my Marks of Passion blame:
Since Jealousie alone can prove,
The surest Witness of my Flame:
And she who without that, a Love can vow,
Believe me, Shepherd, does not merit you.

II.
Then give me leave to doubt, that Fire
I kindle, may another warm:
A Face that cannot move Desire,
May serve at least to end the Charm:
Love else were Witchcraft, that on malice bent,
Denies ye Joys, or makes ye Impotent.

III.
'Tis true, when Cities are on Fire,
Men never wait for Christal Springs;
But to the Neighboring Pools retire;
Which nearest, best Assistance brings;
And serves as well to quench the raging Flame,
As if from God-delighting Streams it came.

IV.
A Fancy strong may do the Feat
Yet this to Love a Riddle is,
And shows that Passion but a Cheat;
Which Men but with their Tongues Confess.
For 'tis a Maxime in Loves learned School,
Who blows the Fire, the flame can only Rule.

V.

Though Honour does your Wish deny,
Honour! the Foe to your Repose;
Yet 'tis more Noble far to dye,
Then break Loves known and Sacred Laws:
What Lover wou'd pursue a single Game,
That cou'd amongst the Fair deal out his flame?

VI.
Since then, Lysander, you desire,
Amynta only to adore;
Take in no Partners to your Fire,
For who well Loves, that Loves one more?
And if such Rivals in your Heart I find,
Tis in My Power to die, but not be kind.

A Dialogue For an Entertainment at Court, Between Damon and Sylvia.

Damon
Ah, Sylvia! if I still pursue,
Whilst you in vain your Scorn improve;
What wonders might your Eies not do:
If they would dress themselves in Love.

Sylvia
Shepherd, you urge my Love in vain,
For I can ne'er Reward your pain;
A Slave each Smile of mine can win,
And all my softning Darts,
When e'er I please, can bring me in
A Thousand Yeilding Hearts.

Damon
Yet if those Slaves you treat with Cruelty,
'Tis an Inglorious Victory;
And those unhappy Swaines you so subdue,
May Learn at last to scorn, as well as you;
Your Beauty though the Gods design'd
Shou'd be Ador'd by all below;
Yet if you want a Godlike Pittying Mind,
Our Adoration soon will colder grow:
'Tis Pitty makes a Deity,
Ah, Silvia! daine to pitty me,
And I will worship none but thee.

Sylvia
Perhaps I may your Councel take,
And Pitty, tho' not Love, for Damons sake;
Love is a Flame my Heart ne'er knew,
Nor knows how to begin to burn for you.

Damon

Ah, Sylvia, who's the happy Swain,
For whom that Glory you ordain!
Has Strephon, Pithius, Hilus, more
Of Youth, of Love, or Flocks a greater store?
My flame pursues you too, with that Address,
Which they want Passion to Profess:
Ah then make some Returns my Charming Shepherdess.

Silvia

Too Faithful Shepherd, I will try my Heart,
And if I can will give you part.

Damon

Oh that was like your self exprest,
Give me but part, and I will steal the rest.

Sylvia

Take care, Young Swain, you treat it well,
If you wou'd have it in your Bosom dwell;
Now let us to the Shades Retreat,
Where all the Nymphs and Shepherds meet.

Damon

And give me there your leave my Pride to show,
For having but the hopes of Conquering you;
Where all the Swaines shall Passion learn of me:
And all the Nymphs to bless like thee.

Silvia

Where every Grace I will bestow,
And every Look and Smile, shall show
How much above the rest I vallue you.

Damon

And I those Blessings will improve;
By constant Faith, and tender Love.

[A Chorus of Satyrs and Nymphs made by another hand.]

On Mr. J. H. In a Fit of Sickness.

I.
If when the God of Day retires,
The Pride of all the Spring decays and dies:
Wanting those Life-begetting Fires
From whence they draw their Excellencies;
Each little Flower hangs down its Gawdy Head,

Losing the Luster which it did Retain;
No longer will its fragrant face be spread,
But Languishes into a Bud again:
So with the Sighing Crowd it fares
Since you, Amyntas, have your Eies withdrawn,
Ours Lose themselves in Silent Tears,
Our days are Melancholy Dawn;
The Groves are Unfrequented now,
The Shady Walks are all Forlorn;
Who still were throng to gaze on you:
With Nymphs, whom your Retirement has undone.

II.
Our Bag-pipes now away are flung,
Our Flocks a Wandering go;
Garlands neglected on the Boughs are hung,
That us'd to adorn each Chearful Brow,
Forsaken looks the enameld May:
And all its wealth Uncourted dies;
Each little Bird forgets its wonted Lay,
That Sung Good Morrow to the welcome Day.
Or rather to thy Lovely Eies.
The Cooling Streams do backward glide:
Since on their Banks they saw not thee,
Losing the Order of their Tide,
And Murmuring chide thy Cruelty;
Then hast to lose themselves i'th' Angry Sea.

III.
Thus every thing in its Degree,
Thy sad Retreat Deplore;
Hast then Amyntas, and Restore;
The whole Worlds Loss in thee.
For like an Eastern Monarch, when you go,
(If such a Fate the World must know)
A Beautious and a Numerous Host
Of Love-sick Maids, will wait upon thy Ghost;
And Death that Secret will Reveal,
Which Pride and Shame did here Conceal;
Live then thou Lovelyest of the Plaines,
Thou Beauty of the Envying Swaines;
Whose Charms even Death it self wou'd court,
And of his Solemn Business make a Sport.

IV.
In Pitty to each Sighing Maid,
Revive, come forth, be Gay and Glad;
Let the Young God of Love implore,
In Pity lend him Darts,
For when thy Charming Eies shall shoot no more;
He'll lose his Title of the God of Hearts.

In Pity to Astrea live,
Astrea, whom from all the Sighing Throng,
You did your oft-won Garlands give:
For which she paid you back in Grateful Song:
Astrea^ who did still the Glory boast,
To be ador'd by thee, and to adore thee most.

V.
With Pride she saw her Rivals Sigh and Pine,
And vainly cry'd, The lovely Youth is mine!
By all thy Charms I do Conjure thee, live;
By all the Joys thou canst receive, and give:
By each Recess and Shade where thou and I,
Loves Secrets did Unfold;
And did the dull Unloving World defy:
Whilst each the Hearts fond Story told.
If all these Conjurations nought Prevail,
Not Prayers or Sighs, or Tears avail,
But Heaven has Destin'd we Deprived must be,
Of so much youth. Wit, Beauty, and of Thee;
I will the Deaf and Angry Powers defie,
Curse thy Decease, Bless thee, and with thee die.

To Lysander, on Some Verses he Writ, and Asking More for His Heart then 'twas Worth.

I.
Take back that Heart, you with such Caution give,
Take the fond valu'd Trifle back;
I hate Love-Merchants that a Trade wou'd drive;
And meanly cunning Bargains make.

II.
I care not how the busy Market goes,
And scorn to Chaffer for a price:
Love does one Staple Rate on all impose,
Nor leaves it to the Traders Choice.

III.
A Heart requires a Heart Unfeign'd and True,
Though Subt'ly you advance the Price.
And ask a Rate that Simple Love ne'er knew:
And the free Trade Monopolize.

IV.
An Humble Slave the Buyer must become
She must not bate a Look or Glance,
You will have all, or you'll have none;
See how Loves Market you inhaunce.

V.
Is't not enough, I gave you Heart for Heart,
But I must add my Lips and Eies;
I must no friendly Smile or Kiss impart;
But you must Dun me with Advice.

VI.
And every Hour still more unjust you grow,
Those Freedoms you my life deny,
You to Adraste are oblig'd to show,
And give her all my Rifled Joy.

VII.
Without Controul she gazes on that Face,
And all the happy Envyed Night,
In the pleas'd Circle of your fond imbrace:
She takes away the Lovers Right.

VIII.
From me she Ravishes those silent hours,
That are by Sacred Love my due;
Whilst I in vain accuse the angry Powers,
That make me hopeless Love pursue.

IX.
Adrastes Ears with that dear Voice are blest,
That Charms my Soul at every Sound,
And with those Love-Inckanting Touches prest:
Which I ne'er felt without a Wound.

X.
She has thee all: whilst I with silent Greif,
The Fragments of thy Softness feel,
Yet dare not blame the happy licenc'd Thief:
That does my Dear-bought Pleasures steal.

XI.
Whilst like a Glimering Taper still I burn,
And waste my self in my own flame,
Adraste takes the welcome rich Return:
And leaves me all the hopeless Pain.

XII.
Be just, my lovely Swain, and do not take
Freedoms you'll not to me allow;
Or give Amynta so much Freedom back:
That she may Rove as well as you.

XIII.
Let us then love upon the honest Square,
Since Interest neither have design'd,

For the sly Gamester, who ne'er plays me fair,
Must Trick for Trick expect to find.

To the Honourable Edward Howard, on His Comedy Called The New Utopia.

I.
Beyond the Merit of the Age,
You have adorn'd the Stage;
So from rude Farce, to Comick Order brought,
Each Action, and each Thought;
To so Sublime a Method, as yet none
(But Mighty Ben alone)
Cou'd e'er arive, and he at distance too;
Were he alive he must resign to you:
You have out-done what e'er he writ,
In this last great Example of your Wit.
Your Solymour does his Morose destroy,
And your Black Page undoes his Barbers Boy.
All his Collegiate Ladies must retire,
While we thy braver Heroins do admire.
This new Utopia rais'd by thee,
Shall stand a Structure to be wondered at,
And men shall cry, this this is he
Who that Poetick City did create:
Of which Moor only did the Model draw,
You did Compleat that little World, and gave it Law.

II.
If you too great a Prospect doe allow
To those whom Ignorance does at distance Seat,
'Tis not to say, the Object is less great,
But they want sight to apprehend it so:
The ancient Poets in their times,
When thro' the Peopl'd Streets they sung their Rhimes,
Found small applause; they sung but still were poor;
Repeated Wit enough at every door.
T'have made 'em demy Gods! but 'twou'd not do,
Till Ages more refin'd esteem'd 'em so.
The Modern Poets have with like Success,
Quitted the Stage, and Sallyed from the Press.
Great Johnson scarce a Play brought forth,
But Monster-like it frighted at its Birth:
Yet he continued still to write,
And still his Satyr did more sharply bite.
He writ tho certain of his Doom,
Knowing his Pow'r in Comedy:
To please a wiser Age to come:
And though he Weapons wore to Justify
The reasons of his Pen; he cou'd not bring

Dull Souls to Sense by Satyr, nor by Cudgelling.

III.
In vain the Errors of the Times,
You strive by wholesom Precepts to Confute,
Not all your Pow'r in Prose or Rhimes,
Can finish the Dispute:
'Twixt those that damn, and those that do admire:
The heat of your Poetick fire.
Your Soul of Thought you may imploy
A Nobler way,
Then in revenge upon a Multitude,
Whose Ignorance only makes 'em rude.
Shou'd you that Justice do,
You must for ever bid adieu,
To Poetry divine,
And ev'ry Muse o'th' Nine:
For Malice then with Ignorance would join,
And so undo the World and You:
So ravish from us that delight,
Of seeing the Wonders which you Write:
And all your Glories unadmir'd must lye,
As Vestal Beauties are Intomb'd before they dye.

IV.
Consider and Consult your Wit,
Despise those Ills you must indure:
And raise your Scorne as great as it,
Be Confident and then Secure.
And let your rich-fraught Pen,
Adventure our again;
Maugre the Stormes that do opose its course,
Stormes that destroy without remorse:
It may new Worlds decry,
Which Peopl'd from thy Brain may know
More than the Universe besides can show:
More Arts of Love, and more of Gallantry.
Write on! and let not after Ages say,
The Whistle or rude Hiss cou'd lay
Thy mighty Spright of Poetry,
Which but the Fools and Guilty fly;
Who dare not in thy Mirror see
Their own Deformity:
Where thou in two, the World dost Character,
Since most of Men Sir Graves, or Peacocks are.

V.
And shall that Muse that did ere while,
Chant forth the Glories of the British Isle,
Shall shee who lowder was than Fame;
Now useless lie, and tame?

Shee who late made the Amazons so Great,
And shee who Conquered Scythia too;
(Which Alexander ne're coud do)
Will you permitt her to retreat?
Silence will like Submission show:
And give Advantage to the Foe!
Undaunted let her once gain appear,
And let her lowdly Sing in every Ear:
Then like thy Mistris Eyes, who have the skill,
Both to preserve and kill;
So thou at once maist be revenged on those
That are thy Foes,
And on thy Friends such Obligations lay,
As nothing but the Deed the Doer can repay.

To Lysander at the Musick Meeting.

It was too much, ye Gods, to see and hear;
Receiving wounds both from the Eye and Ear.
One Charme might have secur'd a Victory,
Both, rais'd the Pleasure even to Extasie:
So Ravisht Lovers in each others Armes,
Faint with excess of Joy, excess of Charmes:
Had I but gaz'd and fed my greedy Eyes,
Perhaps you'd pleas'd no farther than surprize.
That Heav'nly Form might Admiration move,
But, not without the Musick, charm'd with Love:
At least so quick the Conquest had not been:
You storm'd without, and Harmony within:
Nor cou'd I listen to the sound alone,
But I alas must look and was undone:
I saw the Softness that compos'd your Face,
While your Attention heightend every Grace:
Your Mouth all full of Sweetness and Content,
And your fine killing Eyes of Languishment:
Your Bosom now and then a sigh wou'd move,
(For Mustek has the same effects with Love.
Your Body easey and all tempting lay,
Inspiring wishes which the Eyes betray,
In all that have the fate to glance that way:
A careless and a lovely Negligence,
Did a new Charm to every Limb dispence:
So look young Angels, Listening to the sound,
When the Tun'd Spheres Glad all the Heav's around
So Raptur'd lie amidst the wondering Crowc,
So Charmingly Extended on a Cloud.
When from so many ways Loves Arrows storm,
Who can the heedless Heart defend from harm?
Beauty and Musick must the Soul disarme;

Since Harmony, like Fire to Wax, does fit
The softned Heart Impressions to admit:
As the brisk sounds of Warr the Courage move,
Musick prepares and warms the Soul to Love.
But when the kindling Sparks such Fuel meet,
No wonder if the Flame inspired be great.

An Ode to Love.

I.
Dull Love no more thy Senceless Arrows prize,
Damn thy Gay Quiver, break thy Bow;
"Tis only young Lysanders Eyes,
That all the Arts of Wounding know.

II.
A Pox of Foolish Politicks in Love,
A wise delay in Warr the Foe may harme:
By Lazy Siege while you to Conquest move;
His fiercer Beautys vanquish by a Storme.

III.
Some wounded God, to be reveng'd on thee,
The Charming Youth form'd in a lucky houre,
Drest him in all that fond Divinity,
That has out-Rivall'd thee, a God, in Pow'r.

IV.
Or else while thou supinely laid
Basking beneath som Mirtle shade,
In careless sleepe, or tir'd with play,
When all thy Shafts did scatterd ly;
Th'unguarded Spoyles he bore away,
And Arm'd himself with the Artillery.

V.
The Sweetness from thy Eyes he took,
The Charming Dimples from thy Mouth,
That wonderous Softness when you spoke;
And all thy Everlasting Youth.

VI.
Thy bow, thy Quiver, and thy Darts:
Even of thy Painted Wing has rifled thee,
To bear him from his Conquer'd broken Hearts,
To the next Fair and Yeilding She.

Love Reveng'd, A Song.

I.

Cellnda who did Love Disdain,
For whom had languisht many a Swain;
Leading her Bleating Flock to drink,
She spy'd upon the Rivers Brink
A Youth, whose Eyes did well declare,
How much he lov'd, but lov'd not Fer.

II.

At first she Laught, but gaz'd the while,
And soon she lessen'd to a Smile;
Thence to Surprize and Wonder came,
Her Breast to heave, her Heart to flame:
Then cry'd she out, Now, now I prove,
Thou art a God, Almighty Love.

III.

She would have spoke, but shame deny'd,
And bid her first consult her Pride;
But soon she found that Aid was gone;
For Love alas had left her none:
Oh how she burns, but 'tis too late,
For in her Eyes she reads her Fate.

SONG. To a New Scotch Tune.

I.

Young Jemmy was a Lad,
Of Royal Birth and Breeding,
With ev'ry Beauty Clad:
And ev'ry Grace Exceeding;
A face and shape so wondrous fine,
So Charming ev'ry part:
That every Lass upon the Green:
For Jemmy had a Heart.

II.

In Jemmy's Powerful Eyes,
Young Gods of Love are playing,
And on his Face there lies
A Thousand Smiles betraying.
But Oh he dances with a Grace,
None like him e'er was seen;
No God that ever fancy'd was,
Has so Divine a Miene.

III.

To Jemmy ev'ry Swaine
Did lowly doff his Bonnet;
And every Nymph would strain,
To praise him in her Sonnet:
The Pride of all the Youths he was,
The Glory of the Groves,
The Joy of ev'ry tender Lass:
The Theam of all our Loves.

IV.
But Oh Unlucky Fate,
A Curse upon Ambition:
The Busie Fopps of State
Have ruin'd his Condition.
For Glittering Hopes he'as left the Shade,
His Peaceful Hours are gone:
By flattering Knaves and Fools betray'd,
Poor Jemmy is undone.

The Cabal at Nickey Nackeys.

I.
A Pox of the Statesman that's witty,
Who watches and Plots all the Sleepless Night:
For Seditious Harangues, to the Whiggs of the City;
And Maliciously turns a Traytor in Spight.
Let him Wear and Torment his lean Carrion:
To bring his Sham-Plots about,
Till at last King Bishop and Barren,
For the Publick Good he have quite rooted out.

II.
But we that are no Polliticians,
But Rogues that are Impudent, Barefac'd and Great,
Boldly head the Rude Rable in times of Sedition;
And bear all down before us, in Church and in State.
Your Impudence is the best State-Trick;
And he that by Law meanes to rule,
Let his History with ours be related;
And tho' we are the Knaves, we know who's the Fool.

A Paraphrase on the Eleventh Ode. Out of the First Book of Horace.

Dear Silvia, let's no farther strive,
To know how long we have to Live;
Let Busy Gown-men search to know
Their Fates above, while we

Contemplate Beauties greater Power below,
Whose only Smiles give Immortality;
But who seeks Fortune in a Star,
Aims at a Distance much too far,
She's more inconstant than they are. ,
What though this year must be our last,
Faster than Time our Joys let's hast;
Nor think of Ills to come, or past. ,
Give me but Love and Wine, I'll ne'er
Complain my Destiny's severe.
Since Life bears so uncertain Date,
With Pleasure we'll attend our Fate,
And Chearfully go meet it at the Gate. ,
The Brave and Witty know no Fear or Sorrow,
Let us enjoy to day, we'll dye to Morrow.

A Translation.

I.
Lydia, Lovely Maid, more fair
Than Milk or whitest Lilies are,
Than Polisht Indian Iv'ry shows,
Or the fair unblushing Rose.

II.
Open, Maid, thy Locks that hold
Wealth more bright than shining Gold,
Over thy white shoulders laid,
Spread thy Locks, my Charming Maid.

III.
Lydta, ope' thy starry Eyes,
Shew the Beds where Cupid lies,
Open, Maid, thy Rosie-Cheeks,
Red as Sun-declining streaks.

IV.
Shew thy Coral Lips, my Love,
Kiss me softer than the Dove,
Till my Ravish t Soul does lie
Panting in an Ecstasie.

V.
Oh hold and do not pierce my Heart,
Which beats, as life wou'd thence depart
Hide thy Breasts that swell and rise,
Hide 'em from my wishing Eyes.

VI.

Shut thy Bosome, white as Snow,
Whence Arabian perfumes flow;
Hide it from my Raptur'd Touch,
I have gaz'd and kist too much.

VII.
Cruel Maid on Malice bent,
Seest thou not my Languishment?
Lydial Oh I faint! I die!
With thy Beauties Luxury.

A Paraphrase OVID'S Epistle of GENONE to PARIS.

THE ARGUMENT.

Hecuba, being with Child of Paris, dreamed she was delivered of a Firebrand: Priam, consulting the Prophets, was answered the Child should be the Destruction of Troy, wherefore Priam commanded it should be delivered to wild Beasts as soon as born; but Hecuba conveys it secretly to Mount Ida, there to be fostered by the Shepherds, where he falls in love with the Nymph OEnone, but at last being known and ownd, be sails into Greece, and carries Helen to Troy, which OEnone understanding, writes him this Epistle.

To thee, dear Paris, Lord of my Desires,
Once tender Partner of my softest Fires;
To thee I write, mine, while a Shepherd's Swain,
But now a Prince, that Title you disdain.
Oh fatal Pomp, that cou'd so soon divide
What Love, and all our sacred Vows had ty'd!
What God, our Love industrious to prevent,
Curst thee with power, and ruin'd my Content?
Greatness, which does at best but ill agree
With Love, such Distance sets 'twixt Thee and Me.
Whilst thou a Prince, and I a Shepherdess,
My raging Passion can have no redress.
Wou'd God, when first I saw thee, thou hadst been
This Great, this Cruel, Celebrated thing.
That without hope I might have gaz'd and bow'd,
And mixt my Adorations with the Crowd;
Unwounded then I had escap'd those Eyes,
Those lovely Authors of my Miseries.
Not that less Charms their fatal pow'r had drest,
But Fear and Awe my Love had then supprest:
My unambitious Heart no Flame had known,
But what Devotion pays to Gods alone.
I might have wondr'd, and have wisht that He,
Whom Heaven shou'd make me love, might look like Thee.
More in a silly Nymph had been a sin,
This had the height of my Presumption been.
But thou a Flock didst feed on Ida's Plain,

And hadst no Title, but The lovely Swain.
A Title! which more Virgin Hearts has won,
Than that of being own'd King Priam's Son.
Whilst me a harmless Neighbouring Cotager
You saw, and did above the rest prefer.
You saw! and at first sight you lov'd me too,
Nor cou'd I hide the wounds received from you.
Me all the Village Herdsmen strove to gain,
For me the Shepherds sigh'd and su'd in vain,
Thou hadst my heart, and they my cold disdain.
Not all their Offerings, Garlands, and first born
Of their lov'd Ewes, cou'd bribe my Native scorn.
My Love, like hidden Treasure long conceal'd,
Cou'd onely where 'twas destin'd, be reveal'd.
And yet how long my Maiden blushes strove
Not to betray my easie new-born Love.
But at thy sight the kindling Fire wou'd rise,
And I, unskill'd, declare it at my Eyes.
But oh the Joy! the mighty Ecstasie
Possest thy Soul at this Discovery.
Speechless, and panting at my feet you lay,
And short breath'd Sighs told what you cou'd not say.
A thousand times my hand with Kisses prest,
And look'd such Darts, as none cou'd e'er resist.
Silent we gaz'd, and as my Eyes met thine,
New Joy fill'd theirs, new Love and shame fill d mine!
You saw the Fears my kind disorder show'd
And breaking Silence Faith anew you vow'd!
Heavens, how you swore by every Pow r Divine
You wou'd be ever true! be ever mine!
Each God, a sacred witness you invoke,
And wish'd their Curse when e'er these Vows you broke.
Quick to my Heart each perjur'd Accent ran,
Which I took in, believ'd, and was undone.
"Vows are Love's poyson'd Arrows, and the heart
So wounded, rarely finds a Cure from Art.
At least this heart which Fate has destin'd yours,
This heart unpractis'd in Love's mystick pow'rs,
For I am soft and young as April Flowers.

Now uncontroll'd we meet, uncheck'd improve
Each happier Minute in new Joys of Love!
Soft were our hours! and lavishly the Day
We gave intirely up to Love, and Play.
Oft to the cooling Groves our Flocks we led,
And seated on some shaded, flowery Bed,
Watch'd the united Wantons as they fed.
And all the Day my list'ning Soul I hung
Upon the charming Musick of thy Tongue
And never thought the blessed hours too long.
No Swain, no God like thee cou'd ever move,

Or had so soft an Art in whisp'ring Love.
No wonder for thou art Ally'd to Jove!
And when you pip'd, or sung, or danc'd, or spoke,
The God appear'd in every Grace, and Look.
Pride of the Swains, and Glory of the Shades,
The Grief, and Joy of all the Love-sick Maids.
Thus whilst all hearts you rul'd without Controul,
I reign'd the absolute Monarch of your Soul.

Each Beach my Name yet bears, carv'd out by thee,
Paris, and his OEnone fill each Tree;
And as they grow, the Letters larger spread,
Grow still a witness of my Wrongs when dead!

Close by a silent silver Brook there grows
A Poplar, under whose dear gloomy Boughs
A thousand times we have exchanged our Vows!
Oh may'st thou grow! t' an endless date of Years!
Who on thy Bark this fatal Record bears;
When Paris to OEnone proves untrue,
Back Xanthus Streams shall to their Fountains flow.
Turn! turn your Tides! back to your Fountains run!
The perjur'd Swain from all his Faith is gone!

Curst be that day, may Fate appoint the hour,
As Ominous in his black Kalendar;
When Venus, Pallas, and the Wife of Jove
Descended to thee in the Mirtle Grove,
In shining Chariots drawn by winged Clouds:
Naked they came, no Veil their Beauty shrouds;
But every Charm, and Grace expos'd to view,
Left Heav'n to be surveyed, and judg'd by you.
To bribe thy voice Juno wou'd Crowns bestow,
Pallas more gratefully wou'd dress thy Brow
With Wreaths of Wit! Venus propos'd the choice
Of all the fairest Greeks! and had thy Voice.
Crowns, and more glorious Wreaths thou didst despise,
And promis'd Beauty more than Empire prize
This when you told, Gods! what a killing fear
Did over all my shivering Limbs appear?
And I presag'd some ominous Change was near!
The Blushes left my Cheeks, from every part
The Bloud ran swift to guard my fainting heart.
You in my Eyes the glimmering Light perceiv'd
Of parting Life, and on my pale Lips breath'd
Such Vows, as all my Terrors undeceiv'd.
But soon the envying Gods disturb'd our Joy,
Declar'd thee Great! and all my Bliss destroy!

And now the Fleet is Anchor'd in the Bay,
That must to Troy the glorious Youth convey.

Heavens! how you look'd! and what a Godlike Grace
At their first Homage beautify'd your Face!
Yet this no Wonder, or Amazement brought,
You still a Monarch were in Soul, and thought!
Nor cou'd I tell which most the News augments,
Your Joys of Pow'r, or parting Discontents.
You kist the Tears which down my Cheeks did glide,
And mingled yours with the soft falling Tide,
And 'twixt your Sighs a thousand times you said,
Cease, my OEnone! Cease, my charming Maid!
If Paris lives his Native Troy to see,
My lovely Nymph, thou shalt a Princess be!
But my Prophetick Fears no Faith allow'd,
My breaking Heart resisted all you vow'd.
Ah must we part, I cry'd! that killing word
No farther Language coud to Grief afford.
Trembling, I fell upon thy panting Breast,
Which was with equal Love, and Grief opprest,
Whilst sighs and looks, all dying spoke the rest.
About thy Neck my feeble Arms I cast,
Not Vines, nor Ivy circle Elms so fast.
To stay, what dear Excuses didst thou frame.
And fansiedst Tempests when the Seas were calm?
How oft the Winds contrary feign'd to be,
When they, alas, were onely so to me!
How oft new Vows of lasting Faith you swore,
And 'twixt your Kisses all the old run o'er?

But now the wisely Grave, who Love despise.
(Themselves past hope) do busily advise.
Whisper Renown, and Glory in thy Ear,
Language which Lovers fright, and Swains ne'er hear.
For Troy, they cry! these Shepherds Weeds lay down,
Change Crooks for Scepters! Garlands for a Crown!
"But sure that Crown does far less easie sit.
"Than Wreaths of Flow'rs, less innocent and sweet.
"Nor can thy Beds of State so grateful! be,
"As those of Moss, and new fain Leaves with me!

Now tow'rds the Beach we go, and all the way
The Groves, the Fern, dark Woods, and springs survey;
That were so often conscious to the Rites
Of sacred Love, in our dear stoln Delights.
With Eyes all languishing, each place you view,
And signing cry, Adieu, dear Shades, Adieu!
Then 'twas thy Soul e'en doubted which to doe,
Refuse a Crown, or those dear Shades forego!
Glory and Love! the great dispute pursu'd,
But the false Idol soon the God subdu'd.

And now on Board you go, and all the Sails

Are loosned, to receive the flying Gales.
Whilst I, half dead on the forsaken Strand,
Beheld thee sighing on the Deck to stand,
Wafting a thousand Kisses from thy Hand.
And whilst I cou'd the lessening Vessel see,
I gaz'd, and sent a thousand Sighs to thee!
And all the Sea-born Nereids implore
Quick to return thee to our Rustick shore.

Now like a Ghost I glide through ev'ry Grove,
Silent, and sad as Death, about I rove,
And visit all our Treasuries of Love!
This Shade th'account of thousand Joys does hide,
As many more this murmuring Rivers side.
Where the dear Grass, still sacred, does retain
The print, where thee and I so oft have lain.
Upon this Oak thy Pipe, and Garland's plac'd,
That Sicamore is with thy Sheep-hook grac'd.
Here feed thy Flock, once lov'd though now thy scorn,
Like me forsaken, and like me forlorn!

A Rock there is, from whence I cou'd survey
From far the blewish Shore, and distant Sea,
Whose hanging top with toyl I climb'd each day,
With greedy View the prospect I ran o'er,
To see what wish'd for ships approach'd our shore.
One day all hopeless on its point I stood,
And saw a Vessel bounding o'er the Flood,
And as it nearer drew, I cou'd discern
Rich Purple Sails, Silk Cords, and Golden Stern;
Upon the Deck a Canopy was spread
Of Antique work in Gold and Silver made,
Which mix'd with Sun-beams dazling Light display'd.
But oh! beneath this glorious Scene of State
(Curst be the sight) a fatal Beauty sate.
And fondly you were on her Bosome lay'd,
Whilst with your perjur'd Lips her Fingers play'd;
Wantonly curl'd and dally'd with that hair,
Of which, as sacred Charms, I Bracelets wear.

Oh! hadst thou seen me then in that mad state,
So ruin'd, so desig'd for Death and Fate,
Fix'd on a Rock, whose horrid Precipice
In hollow Murmurs wars with Angry Seas;
Whilst the bleak Winds aloft my Garments bear,
Ruffling my careless and dishevel'd hair,
I look'd like the sad Statue of Despair.
With out-strech'd voice I cry'd, and all around
The Rocks and Hills my dire complaints resound.
I rent my Garments, tore my flattering Face,
Whose false deluding Charms my Ruine was.

Mad as the Seas in Storms, I breathe Despair,
Or Winds let loose in unresisting Air.
Raging and Frantick through the Woods I fly,
And Paris! lovely, faithless Paris cry.
But when the Echos sound thy Name again,
I change to new variety of Pain.
For that dear name such tenderness inspires,
And turns all Passion to Loves softer Fires:
With tears I fall to kind Complaints again,
So Tempests are allay'd by Show'rs of Rain.

Say, lovely Youth, why wou'dst thou thus betray
My easie Faith, and lead my heart astray?
I might some humble Shepherd's Choice have been,
Had I that Tongue ne'er heard, those Eyes ne'er seen.
And in some homely Cott, in low Repose,
Liv'd undisturb'd with broken Vows and Oaths:
All day by shaded Springs my Flocks have kept,
And in some honest Arms at night have slept
Then unupbraided with my wrongs thou'dst been
Safe in the Joys of the fair Grecian Queen:
What Stars do rule the Great? no sooner you
Became a Prince, but you were Perjur'd too
Are Crowns and Falshoods then consistent things?
And must they all be faithless who are Kings?
The Gods be prais'd that I was humbly born,
Even tho it renders me my Paris scorn.
For I had rather this way wretched prove,
Than be a Queen and faithless in my Love.
Not my fair Rival wou'd I wish to be,
To come prophan'd by others Joys to thee.
A spotless Maid into thy Arms I brought,
Untouch'd in Fame, ev'n Innocent in thought;
Whilst she with Love has treated many a Guest,
And brings thee but the leavings of a Feast:
With Theseus from her Country made Escape,
Whilst she miscall'd the willing Flight, a Rape.
So now from Atreus Son, with thee is fled,
And still the Rape hides the Adult'rous Deed.
And is it thus Great Ladies keep intire
That Vertue they so boast, and you admire?
Is this a Trick of Courts, can Ravishment
Serve for a poor Evasion of Consent?
Hard shift to save that Honour priz'd so high,
Whilst the mean Fraud's the greater Infamy.
How much more happy are we Rural Maids,
Who know no other Palaces than Shades?
Who wish no Title to inslave the Croud,
Lest they shou'd babble all our Crimes aloud;
No Arts our Good to shew, our Ill to hide
Nor know to cover faults of Love with Pride.

I lov'd, and all Love's Dictates did pursue,
And never thought it cou'd be Sin with you.
To Gods, and Men, I did my Love proclaim;
For one soft hour with thee, my charming Swain,
Wou'd Recompence an Age to come of Shame,
Cou'd it as well but satisfie my Fame.
But oh! those tender hours are fled and lost,
And I no more of Fame, or Thee can boast!
'Twas thou wert Honour, Glory, all to me:
Till Swains had learn'd the Vice of Perjury,
No yielding Maids were charg'd with Infamy.
'Tis false and broken Vows make Love a Sin,
Hadst thou been true, We innocent had been.
But thou less faith than Autumn leaves do'st show,
Which ev'ry Blast bears from their native Bough.
Less Weight, less Constancy, in thee is born,
Than in the slender mildew'd Ears of Corn.
Oft when you Garlands wove to deck my hair,
Where mystick Pinks, and Dazies mingled were,
You swore 'twas fitter Diadems to bear:
And when with eager Kisses prest my hand,
Have said, How well a Scepter 'twould command!
And when I danc'd upon the Flow'ry Green,
With charming, wishing Eyes survey my Mien,
And cry! the Gods design'd thee for a Queen!
Why then for Helen dost thou me forsake?
Can a poor empty Name such difference make?
Besides if Love can be a Sin, thine's one,
To Menclaus Helen does belong.
Be Just, restore her back, She's none of thine,
And, charming Paris, thou art onely mine.
'Tis no Ambitious Flame that makes me sue
To be again belov'd, and blest by you;
No vain desire of being ally'd t' a King,
Love is the onely Dowry I can bring,
And tender Love is all I ask again;
Whilst on her dang'rous Smiles fierce War must wait
Witli Fire and Vengeance at your Palace gate,
Rouze your soft Slumbers with their rough Alarms,
And rudely snatch you from her faithless Arms:
Turn then, fair Fugitive, e'er 'tis too late,
E'er thy mistaken Love procures thy Fate;
E'er a wrong'd Husband does thy Death design,
And pierce that dear, that faithless Heart of thine.

APHRA BEHN – A SHORT BIOGRAPHY

Aphra Behn was baptised on December 14th in 1640.

Although she was a prolific and well established writer in her own lifetime facts about her remain scant and difficult to confirm. What can safely be said though is that Aphra Behn is now regarded as a key English playwright and a major figure in Restoration theatre

In fact even where and to whom she was born are subject to discussion.

According to which account you read – and there are many – Aphra was born in Harbledown, near Canterbury. Another that she was born to a barber, John Amis and his wife Amy. Or again she was born to a couple named Cooper.

In the "The Histories And Novels of the Late Ingenious Mrs. Behn" (1696) it is written that Aphra was born to Bartholomew Johnson, a barber, and Elizabeth Denham, a wet-nurse. However a claim by Colonel Thomas Colepeper, who states he knew her as a child, wrote in Adversaria that she was born at "Sturry or Canterbury" to a Mr Johnson and that she had a sister named Frances. Anne Kingsmill Finch, Countess of Winchilsea, a poetic contemporary, says that Aphra was born in Wye in Kent, and was the 'Daughter to a Barber.'

None of these accounts can be relied upon and it follows that with so few facts the early part of her life cannot be clearly illustrated.

However what can be accurately suggested is that Aphra was born in the rising tensions to the English Civil War. Obviously a time of much division and difficulty as the King and Parliament, and their respective forces, came ever closer to conflict.

But still facts do not reveal themselves in any quantity. As a young woman a version exists of Aphra's journeying to Surinam with Bartholomew Johnson. He was said to have died on the journey, leaving his wife and children spending some months in the country. It is during this trip that Aphra claims to have met an African slave leader. These experiences formed the basis for one of her most famous works, "Oroonoko". In "Oroonoko" Behn Aphra gifts herself the position of narrator and her first biographer accepted the proposition that Aphra was indeed the daughter of the lieutenant general of Surinam, as in the story. There is little evidence to support this case, and none of her contemporaries acknowledge this, or any, aristocratic status. There is also no evidence that Oroonoko existed as an actual person or that any such slave revolt, is anything but an invention.

However it is possible that she acted a spy in the colony. Possibilities exist. Perhaps Aphra re-wrote her own history as and when it suited her needs at the time.

The common method of gathering information in these times was Church records and for a few, tax records. Aphra Behn is mentioned in neither. As well as Aphra Behn or Mrs Behn she was, at times, also known as Ann Behn, Mrs Bean, agent 160 and Astrea.

Shortly after her supposed return to England from Surinam in 1664, Aphra may have married Johan Behn (also written as Johann and John Behn). He could have been a merchant of German or Dutch extraction, possibly from Hamburg. He died or the couple separated that same year, however from this point we can be sure Aphra used the title "Mrs Behn" as her professional name.

There is some suggestion that Aphra may have been a Catholic or at least leaned towards this school of faith. She once commented that she was "designed for a nun." Many of those around her were Catholic, such as Henry Neville who was later arrested for his Catholicism, and this would have aroused suspicions during the anti-Catholic fervour of the 1680s. She was a monarchist, and her sympathy for the Stuarts, and particularly for the Catholic Duke of York may be demonstrated by her dedication of her play "The Rover, Part II" to him after he had been exiled for the second time. Aphra was dedicated to the restored King Charles II. As political parties emerged during this time, Aphra became a Tory supporter.

By 1666 Aphra had become attached to the court. Domestically the Plague was sweeping the Nation and the Great Fire was about to erupt through London. In foreign affairs England and the Netherlands had engaged in The Second Anglo-Dutch War from 1665. Aphra was recruited as a political spy in Antwerp on behalf of King Charles II, possibly in league with Thomas Killigrew.

This is probably the beginning of more accurate records on Aphra's life. Her code name is said to have been Astrea (though there are others), a name under which she later published many of her writings. Her chief duty was to establish a relationship with William Scot, son of Thomas Scot, a regicide who had been executed in 1660. Scot was believed to be ready to become a spy in the English service and to report on the activities of the English exiles who were thought to be plotting against the King. Aphra arrived in Bruges in July 1666 with a mission to secure Scot into a double agent, but there is evidence that Scot would betray her to the Dutch.

Aphra however found life as a spy not quite the romantic interlude that many assume would be the case. She arrived unprepared; the cost of living shocked her, and after a month, she had to pawn her jewellery. King Charles was slow in paying, either for her services or for her expenses whilst abroad. She had to borrow money so she could return to London, where she spent a year petitioning King Charles for payment unsuccessfully. A short while later a warrant was issued for her arrest, but little to suggest it was actually served or that she went to prison for her debt.

The death of her husband and her debts seemed to push her towards a more sustainable and substantial career. Aphra began work for the King's Company and the Duke's Company players as a scribe. These were, in fact, the only two licensed theatre groups in London. The theatres had been closed under Cromwell and were now re-opening under Charles II and a more liberal atmosphere. Theatre technology was being imported from Europe and being integrated into the staging of some plays. It was a great moment on which to embark upon a career in theatre.

Aphra who had previously only written poetry now embarked on such a career. Her first, "The Forc'd Marriage", was staged in 1670, followed by "The Amorous Prince" (1671). After her third play, "The Dutch Lover", fails to please Aphra had a three year lull in her writing career. Again it is speculated that she went travelling again, possibly once again as a spy.

After this sojourn her writing moves towards comic works, which prove commercially more successful. Her most popular works included "The Rover" and "Love-Letters Between a Nobleman and His Sister" (1684–87).

With her growing reputation Aphra became friends with many of the most notable writers of the day. This is The Age of Dryden and his literary dominance. As well as his friendship she includes also those of Elizabeth Barry, John Hoyle, Thomas Otway and Edward Ravenscroft, and was also attached to the circle of the Earl of Rochester.

Aphra often used her plays to attack the parliamentary Whigs claiming, "In public spirits call'd, good o' th' Commonwealth... So tho' by different ways the fever seize...in all 'tis one and the same mad disease." This was Aphra's criticism to parliament which had denied the king funds.

From the mid 1680's Aphra's health began to decline. This was exacerbated by her continual state of debt and descent into poverty.

In 1687 she published A Discovery of New Worlds, a translation of a French popularisation of astronomy, Entretiens sur la pluralité des mondes, by Bernard le Bovier de Fontenelle, written as a novel in a form similar to her own work, but w th her new, religiously oriented preface.

As her end approached in 1689 it became increasingly hard for her to even hold a pen though her desire to continue to write was unquenchable. In her final days, she wrote the translation of the final book of Abraham Cowley's Six Books of Plants.

Aphra Behn died on April 16th 1689, and is buried in the East Cloister of Westminster Abbey. The inscription on her tombstone reads: "Here lies a Proof that Wit can never be Defence enough against Mortality." She was quoted as stating that she had led a "life dedicated to pleasure and poetry."

Her legacy is broad. Firstly as a woman she broke down many of the barriers which regarded only men as writers, especially in the commercial arena. In all she would write and have performed 19 plays, contribute to more, and become one of the first prolific, high-profile female dramatists in these Isles.

In her own golden age of the 1670s and 1680s she was one of the most productive playwrights in Britain, second only to the immense talents of the Poet Laureate John Dryden.

Much of her work has been criticised for its bawdy tone as well as its masculine form but needs must and she was working to live, to survive, and to widen her spread as an author.

She received widespread support from many other successful writers including Thomas Otway, Nahum Tate (also a Poet Laureate), Jacob Tonson, Nathaniel Lee and Thomas Creech.

Aphra is now rightly seen as a key dramatist of the seventeenth-century theatre. Her prose vitally important to the on-going development of the English novel.

Following Aphra's death new female dramatists such as 'Ariadne', Delarivier Manley, Mary Pix, Susanna Centlivre and Catherine Trotter acknowledged Behn as an inspiration who opened up the public space for women writers to be accepted.

In succeeding centuries her appreciation has been volatile. For instance in the morally reserved Victorian clime both the writer and her works were ignored or dismissed as indecent. The Victorian novelist and critic Julia Kavanagh wrote, "the disgrace of Aphra Behn is that, instead of raising man to woman's moral standard, she sank woman to the level of man's coarseness".

However by the 20th century, however, Aphra's fame was back in fashion. Since then her works have been well appreciated and her place in our literary pantheon assured.

APHRA BEHN – A CONCISE BIBLIOGRAPHY

Plays
The Forced Marriage (1670)
The Amorous Prince (1671)
The Dutch Lover (1673)
Abdelazer (1676)

The Town Fop (1676)
The Rover, Part I (1677)
Sir Patient Fancy (1678)
The Feigned Courtesans (1679)
The Young King (1679)
The False Count (1681)
The Rover, Part II (1681)
The Roundheads (1681)
The City Heiress (1682)
Like Father, Like Son (1682)
Prologue and Epilogue to Romulus and Hersilia, or The Sabine War (November 1682)
The Lucky Chance (1686) with composer John Blow
The Emperor of the Moon (1687)
The Widow Ranter (1689)
The Younger Brother (1696)

Novels
The Fair Jilt
Agnes de Castro
Love-Letters Between a Nobleman and His Sister (1684)
Oroonoko (1688)

Short Stories
The Fair Jilt (1688)
The History of the Nun: or, the Fair Vow-Breaker (1688)
The History of the Servant
The Lover-Boy of Germany
The Girl Who Loved the German Lover-Boy

Poetry Collections
Poems upon Several Occasions, with A Voyage to the Island of Love (1684)
Lycidus; or, The Lover in Fashion (1688)

www.ingramcontent.com/pod-product-compliance
Lightning Source LLC
Chambersburg PA
CBHW060139050426
42448CB00010B/2198